THE WOMAN'S
BOOK OF PRAYER

365 Blessings, Poems
and Meditations

Becca Anderson

mango
PUBLISHING

CORAL GABLES

Cover Design: Jermaine Lau
Layout & Design: Katia Mena
Interior Illustrations: AdobeStock (Nessa, Kara-Kotsya)

For permission requests, please contact the publisher at:
Mango Publishing Group
2850 S Douglas Road, 2nd Floor
Coral Gables, FL 33134 USA
info@mango.bz

For special orders, quantity sales, course adoptions and corporate sales, please email the publisher at sales@mango.bz. For trade and wholesale sales, please contact Ingram Publisher Services at customer.service@ingramcontent.com or +1.800.509.4887.

The Woman's Book of Prayer: 365 Blessings, Poems and Meditations

Library of Congress Cataloging-in-Publication number: 2018965823
ISBN: (print) 978-1-63353-777-4, (ebook) 978-1-63353-802-3
BISAC category code: REL012020, RELIGION / Christian Living / Devotional

Printed in the United States of America

To my mother, Helen, who taught me to pray. Love eternal.

"Saying 'thank you' creates love."

—Daphne Rose Kingma

Table of Contents

Foreword

How Do Women Pray?

Women's prayers take many forms—some obvious, others subtle…
and occasionally surprising.

We bow our heads and close our eyes as we pray for blessings,
protection, and healing. Often, we drop to our knees as we seek
to know God's will. Sometimes we look *up*—to the clouds, to the
moon, to the sunrise or sunset, to find spiritual connection with
Heaven above.

Many of us quiet our bodies and our minds in meditation—searching
for our higher selves, the indwelling God, the inherent goodness that
resides deep inside.

And perhaps most importantly, we often gather with kindred spirits,
fellow seekers, to pray in community—for we know that the Kingdom
of God isn't just *within* us, it is *among* us. Wherever two or more
are gathered, God is there. We find the wisdom, guidance, security,
strength, insight, meaning, comfort, and love that we yearn for
whenever we pray together.

This slender volume you hold in your hands is a wonderful collection
of prayers by and for women—old and young, from many walks
of life, from near and far, from past and present. In gathering this
collection, the author invites you to add your own prayers, too.

In joy!

BJ Gallagher
Author of *If God Is Your Co-Pilot, Switch Seats* and
coauthor of *Your Life Is Your Prayer*

Introduction

I once had the pleasure of attending a talk by Huston Smith, a preeminent scholar of the world's religions who first came to the attention of the world when he brought a young Tibetan Buddhist monk—His Holiness the Dalai Lama—to America for the first time. Smith spoke about the continuing impact of religion in our world, most notably, the strife in the Middle East over religious differences. He was at his most joyous when he described his own spiritual practices to us. They were beautiful in their simplicity. Smith said that, upon rising each day, he did Hatha yoga for some minutes followed by reading a few pages of sacred text, after which he meditated or prayed for at least five minutes. He would finish his morning ritual by doing a bit of yard work and some composting, which resulted in rich, dark soil and a beautiful garden that he greatly enjoyed.

The entire audience smiled as they listened to this great and humble man describe the simple spiritual practices with which he began each day. These were Huston Smith's personal morning rituals. I loved the irony that this premier academic, who has such a deep understanding of all the religious rituals throughout history, had created such an uncomplicated practice for himself. I left the talk inspired and soon felt compelled to gather prayers that could bring meaning into our lives.

Whether people are conscious of it or not, our lives are centered upon daily ritual. Prayer is one of the most important of our human rituals. The Wednesday night pizza and movie with the kids is a family ritual. It could be greatly enriched by adding a spiritual aspect—perhaps children could share the highlight of their week so far, and photos or memories could be added to a family album to be treasured for generations to come. A prayer of grace should happen before the breaking of bread in the form of pizza, too! The Saturday night date is a romantic ritual, knitting circles are a growing trend, and doing yoga is replacing going to the gym as a spiritual and physical workout. People need ceremony to inform and enrich their lives, to deal with stress, and above all, to create meaning in their lives.

Although I was brought up as a First Day Adventist, when I studied history, I kept discovering global prayers and practices from the past that I felt were just as relevant today. The beauty of knowing history is that we can learn from the past and take the best to heart by applying it to our lives. Various approaches to prayer are very much a part of our history and should be studied and applied to our lives today. Prayer gets us out of or heads and back into our bodies. It gets us into a place of spirit. By praying every day, you can grow in wisdom and feel an increasing sense of your aliveness. At the end of this book, I am including the guide that my Gratitude and Grace Prayer Circle used to start our gatherings. I can tell you it works, as we have gotten each other through illness, divorce, pregnancy, sick children, loss of parents, widowhood, job loss, financial crises, and a lot of weddings, babies, holidays, and happy days. Honestly, I don't know where I would be without this prayerful sisterhood and the deep bonds of love and spirit.

Many blessings to you and yours!

Becca Anderson

Chapter One

January:
New Year, New Beginnings,
New You

"The beginning is always today."

—Mary Wollstonecraft

"The most difficult thing is the decision to act, the rest is merely tenacity. The fears are paper tigers. You can do anything you decide to do."

—Amelia Earhart

"An exciting and inspiring future awaits you beyond the noise in your mind, beyond the guilt, doubt, fear, shame, insecurity, and heaviness of the past you carry around."

—Debbie Ford

"Never underestimate the power of dreams and the influence of the human spirit. We are all the same in this notion: The potential for greatness lives within each of us."

—Wilma Rudolph

"Take a breath, and when you do, realize that you can make all your dreams come true: Wish upon the breeze that softly blows Think about the steps that on your path you must go Send your intentions back upon the wind And get ready to pick up the journey to your dreams again."

—Jasmeine Moonsong

1
Rise Up, O Woman of God

Rise Up, O Woman of God
In what He has given you,
The things God has laid on your heart,
Rise up, go forth, and do
Unlock what God has placed within,
The potential you have inside
The world is waiting for your release
To expand your wings and fly.

—M.S. Lowndes

2
Cast Your Mind Forward

The future is made of the same stuff as the present.

—Simone Weil

3
Flying to New Heights

If you wish to fly to new heights,
begin by setting your sights
on a destination you can reach
and then create a flight plan,
a map, that will be your guide.

—Debbie Ford

4

Dreaming and Doing

Without leaps of imagination,
or dreaming,
we lose the excitement of possibilities.
Dreaming, after all,
is a form of planning.

—Gloria Steinem

5

A Parable of the Mustard Seed

Never lose an opportunity
of urging a practical beginning,
however small, for it is wonderful
how often in such matters
the mustard-seed germinates
and roots itself.

—Florence Nightingale

6

Gratitude to the Heavens Above

Thank you, God, for this new day, for the life you are giving each
member of my family: Thank you for (name each member of the
immediate family, not forgetting yourself). Bless each one of us with
the strength and health we need to serve you today, with the joy we
need not to give in to discouragement, anger, or boredom, with the

protection we need against physical and moral danger, and with the love we need to give hope to those we meet.

—Unknown

7
Look Out for Those Miracles

The new always happens against the overwhelming odds of statistical laws and their probability, which for all practical, everyday purposes amounts to certainty; the new therefore always appears in the guise of a miracle.

—Hannah Arendt

8
The Sustainer of All

You alone are God,
You were from of old,
And You will be until eternity, always, first and last,
Now and always for ever and ever.
As for You, You are the same,
and Your epoch will not come to an end;
As for You, You are the same,
and Your kingdom will not be abolished,
And Your Power is invincible,
And Your strength is untiring,
And Your magnificence will not be humbled,
And the splendor of Your Name will not be dispelled,
and the praise of Your exalted fame will not be diminished,

And Your light will not be darkened,
And Your decree will not be abrogated,
The pillar of Your word will not be overthrown,
And Your wisdom will not fall into error,
And Your counsel will not be concealed.
You alone are God, God of all;

—Ethiopian Hassidic Prayer

9

Rejuvenation

With arms outstretched I thank.
With heart beating gratefully I love.
With body in health I jump for joy.
With spirit full I live.

—Terri Guillemets

10

Inspiration and Aspiration

Far away there in the sunshine
are my highest aspirations.
I may not reach them,
but I can look up and see their beauty,
believe in them, and try to follow
where they lead.

—Louisa May Alcott

Prayer Practice: Ritual Cleansing, Purification

Many religions and cultures have their own forms of ritual cleansings (Baptisms/Christenings, Mikveh, Ghusl/Wudu, Snanam, etc.) that each have different symbolic meanings. Though many of these ritual baths are purely spiritual, some have also incorporated material objects for both physical and metaphysical cleansing; for instance, the Romans used oils and fragrances, Indians used herbs and spices, and even Cleopatra added milk and honey to her ritual baths. These rituals are typically used to mark a rebirth or significant change in one's life and are often believed to have purifying properties. While some of these ancient rituals have come under criticism by women for suggesting that women are unclean, modern feminists have reclaimed spiritual bathing as a way to appreciate femininity and oneself. Any woman can incorporate the idea of ritual cleansing into her life in many forms either similar to or symbolizing the original concepts. Taking a meditative bath with your favorite oils and candles, cleaning out your house, or even deleting toxic friends from social media can all be compared to the cleansing and rebirth that is at the core of these ritual ceremonies.

11

Arise in Radiance and Go Down in Joy

The earth is full of your goodness,
your greatness and understanding,
your wisdom and harmony.
How wonderful are the lights that you created.
You formed them with strength and power
and they shine very wonderfully on the world,
magnificent in their splendor.
They arise in radiance and go down in joy.
Reverently they fulfill your divine will.
They are tributes to your name
as they exalt your sovereign rule in song.

—Ancient Hebrew Hymn, 516 BC

12

Cycles

When you arise in the morning, think of what a precious privilege
it is to be alive—to breathe, to think, to enjoy, to love—then make
that day count!

—Brenda Knight

13
The Rewards of Risk

It is so easy to close down to risk, to protect ourselves against change
and growth. But no baby bird emerges without first destroying
the perfect egg sheltering it. We must risk being raw and fresh and
awkward. For without such openness, life will not penetrate us anew.
Unless we are open, we will not be filled.

—Patricia Monaghan

14
Hearing the Music of the World

How wonderful, O Lord, are the works of your hands!
The heavens declare Your glory,
the arch of the sky displays Your handiwork
In Your love You have given us the power
to behold the beauty of Your world
robed in all its splendor.
The sun and the stars, the valleys and the hills,
the rivers and the lakes all disclose Your presence.
The roaring breakers of the sea tell of Your awesome might,
the beasts of the field and the birds of the air
bespeak Your wondrous will.
In Your goodness You have made us able to hear
the music of the world.
The voices of the loved ones
reveal to us that You are in our midst.
A divine voice sings through all creation.

—Ancient Jewish Prayer

15

A Perfect Love

AND GOD SAID TO THE SOUL:
I desired you before the world began.
I desire you now as you desire me.
And where the desires of two come together
The love is perfected.

—Mechthild of Megberg, Thirteenth Century Nun

16

The Day Is Done

Even here in America,
we felt the cool, refreshing breeze of freedom.
When Nelson Mandela took the seat of Presidency in his country
where formerly he was not even allowed to vote
we were enlarged by tears of pride,
as we saw Nelson Mandela's former prison guards invited,
courteously, by him to watch from the front rows his inauguration.
We saw him accept the world's award in Norway
with the grace and gratitude
of the Solon in Ancient Roman Courts,
and the confidence of African Chiefs from ancient royal stools.
No sun outlasts its sunset,
but it will rise again and bring the dawn.

—Maya Angelou

17

The Joy in a Heart That Beats

Peace.
Peace, She says to me.
Peace to your soul.
I am the beauty in the leaf.
I am the echo in a baby's laugh.
I am your Mother.
I am the joy in the heart that beats.
I am the free woman.
I am the one who breaks the shackles of oppression.
You are my hands and feet.

—Gaian Prayer

18

Live the Life That Is Given to You

Your life is the only opportunity
that life can give you.
If you ignore it,
if you waste it,
you will only turn to dust.

—Rab'ia al-Adawiyya

19
Help Me Live a New Life

Dear Lord God,
cover my sins and guilt
with the righteousness
of your Son, my Savior.
Create in me a pure heart
and help me live a new life in you!
Amen.

—Jes Woller

20
Rite of the Righteous Woman

Dear God, please make us dangerous women.
May we be women who acknowledge our power to change,
and grow, and be radically alive for God.
May we be healers of wounds and righters of wrongs.
May we weep with those who weep and speak for those
who cannot speak for themselves.
May we cherish children, embrace the elderly, and empower the poor.
May we pray deeply and teach wisely.
May we be strong and gentle leaders.
May we sing songs of joy and talk down fear.
May we never hesitate to let passion push us, conviction
compel us, and righteous anger energize us.
May we strike fear into all that is unjust and evil in the world.

May we dismantle abusive systems and silence lies with truth.
May we shine like stars in a darkened generation.

—Solano Sisterhood

21

Faith, Hope, and Charity

The pow'r that comes when sinking low
To man who grasps for straw or rope,
Will clutch til has he breathe no more
For where there's life, there's hope.
If my good turn be given to
My fellow man's deficiency,
I'll try to share my lowly gifts
Of Faith and Hope and Charity.

—Anne Shannon Demarest

22

Grace of Our Mother

Hail Mary, full of grace.
The Lord is with thee.
Blessed art thou amongst women,
and blessed is the fruit of thy womb, Jesus.
Holy Mary, Mother of God,
pray for us sinners,
now and at the hour of our death.
Amen.

—Catholic Holy Rosary

23

Living in Peace

Come, Spirit,
make me docile to your voice.
Help me debate angels.
Let your will be done in me
even if it means
misunderstanding,
rejection,
scandal.
Give me wisdom to find you
in the irrational:
heavens gone awry,
astrologers' predictions,
Give me such hospitality of heart that
songs in the night.
family,
foreign seers,
poor shepherds and animals
find a home in my presence.

—Benedictine Sisters

24

Who Made the World?

I don't know exactly what a prayer is.
I do know how to pay attention, how to fall down
into the grass, how to kneel down in the grass,
how to be idle and blessed, how to stroll through the fields,

which is what I have been doing all day.
Tell me, what else should I have done?
Doesn't everything die at last, and too soon?
Tell me, what is it you plan to do
with your one wild and precious life?

—Mary Oliver

25

Let There Be Peace and Justice for All Creation

Let us see one another through eyes
enlightened by understanding and compassion.
Empower us to be instruments of justice
and equality everywhere.

—Jean Shinoda Bolen

26

Invocation for Future Generations

Divine Earth—bring greening and surety to the world.
Like the stretching branches of the tree,
May we stretch ourselves
Into the life-affirming paths of reconciliation and healing.
Like the deep peaceful dome of night,
May we stand firm in the Goddess and the God,
Through this "dark night" of confusion and fear, and false "stars."
May our souls be strong, steady, and revealing.

May our spirits be enlightened, faithful, and sure.
May our choices be wise and enduring for the generations to come.

—Pashta Marymoon

27
Just Believe

Faith is the first factor
in a life devoted to service.
Without it, nothing is possible.
With it, nothing is impossible.

—Mary McLeod Bethune

28
A Life of Service Is a Holy Life

Make us worthy, Lord, to serve our fellow men
throughout the world who live and die in poverty and hunger.
Give them through our hands this day their daily bread,
and by our understanding love, give peace and joy.

—Mother Teresa (St. Teresa of Calcutta)

29
Rivers of Happiness

May the winds bring us happiness.
May the rivers carry happiness to us.
May the plants give us happiness.
May night and day yield us happiness.

May the dust of the earth bring us happiness.
May the heavens give us happiness.
May the trees give us happiness.
May the sun pour down happiness.

—Taittirya Aranyaka

30
Find Courage and Comfort in the Everyday

Wage peace with your breath.
Wage peace with your listening: hearing sirens, pray loud.
Remember your tools: flower seeds, clothes pins, clean rivers.
Make soup.
Play music, memorize the words for thank you in three languages.

—Judyth Hill

31
When Times Are Hard, Create Something

Children, everybody, here's what to do during war:
In a time of destruction, create something.
A poem.
A parade.
A community.
A school.
A vow.
A moral principle. One peaceful moment.

—Maxine Hong Kingston

Wise Words: Women Are Creating the Future

"Every achievement, big or small, begins in your mind."

—Mary Kay Ash

"This has always been a motto of mine: Attempt the impossible in order to improve your work."

—Bette Davis

"You are the one that possesses the keys to your being. You carry the passport to your own happiness."

—Diane von Furstenberg

"The future depends entirely on what each of us does every day; a movement is only people moving."

—Gloria Steinem

Chapter Two

February:
Learning to Love Yourself in the Same Way You Love All Others

"I am my own muse, the subject I know best."

—Frida Kahlo

"We have all a better guide in ourselves, if we would attend to it, than any other person can be."

—Jane Austen

"Caring for myself is not self-indulgence, it is self-preservation, and that is an act of political warfare."

—Audre Lorde

"Always be a first-rate version of yourself, instead of a second-rate version of somebody else."

—Judy Garland

"You've gotta do things that make you happy. As women, we tend to give away a lot. We take care of a lot of people, and we can't forget to take care of ourselves."

—Jennifer Lopez

32

You Are a Child of God

You are an eternal being of light and love. You are a child of God,
and abundance is your inheritance. You are at a deep level one with
the whole universe, and therefore everything you need already exists
within you. Everything!

—Cissi Williams

33

Women Helping Women

my heart aches for sisters more than anything it aches for women
helping women
like flowers ache for spring

—rupi kaur

34

The Eternal Truth from the Hugging Saint

When someone is full of Love and Compassion,
he cannot draw a line between
two countries, two faiths, or two religions.

—Amma

35

Do You Know How Great You Are?

Most women secretly believe that they are 'not enough.' The very opposite is true. You are way…WAY more than enough. You have more than enough to do, be, create, and have everything you desire! In order to have EVERYTHING you desire, you must shift your beliefs and begin to see yourself in a new and strong way. It's about creating a powerful mindset shift…the first step is connecting with your Inner Goddess.

—Lisa Marie Rosati

36

Answers to Heal Our Deepest Wounds

Within ourselves, there are voices that provide us with all the answers that we need to heal our deepest wounds, to transcend our limitations, to overcome our obstacles or challenges, and to see where our soul is longing to go.

—Debbie Ford

37

We Are All Born Good, We Are All Born Different

Ren zhi chu
Xing ben shan
Xing xiang jin
Xi xiang yuan
Gou bu jiao
Xing nai qian
Jiao zhi dao
Gui yi zhuan

—

When a child is born,
At the root, is good.
Everyone's nature is the same
But everyone experiences different things.
If there is no Way,
We will move away from our nature.
The teaching of the Way
Is valuable because it is particular to each [woman and] man.

—Thirteenth Century Southern Chinese Poem

38

Let Us Exult in the Sheer Delight of Being Alive

What, you ask, is the beginning of it all?
And it is this…
Existence that multiplied itself for sheer delight of being

and plunged into numberless trillions of forms
so that it might find itself innumerably.

—Sri

39
Still Awareness

I believe it is the most important.
It is our most unique gift. It is perhaps the greatest gift we can give.
In our language this quality is called *dadirri*.
It is inner, deep listening and quiet, still awareness…
When I experience *dadirri*,
I am made whole again.
I can sit on the river bank or walk through the trees;
even if someone close to me has passed away,
I can find my peace in this silent awareness.
There is no need of words…
It is just being aware…

—Miriam-Rose Ungunmerr-Bauman, Aboriginal Artist & Teacher

40
Healing Touch

Touch the pain of the world
and release hope into the darkness.

—Sister Simone Campbell, Sisters of Social Service

41
Have Faith in Yourself, Too

If the whole universe can be found in our own body and mind, this is where we need to make our inquiries. We all have the answers within ourselves, we just have not got in touch with them yet. The potential of finding the truth within requires faith in ourselves.

—Ayya Khema

42
Let Us Love One Another

Together we travel the ongoing concentric spiral
knowing that we are loving to know how loving we are.
We are loving to know how loving we are.
Knowing that we are loving.
Loving to know how.
How loving we are to know.
We are loving to know how loving we are.

—Amy Leader

43
Everything You Need to Know Is Inside You

The answer lies within ourselves. If we can't find peace and happiness there, it's not going to come from the outside.

—Tenzin Palmo

44

Love Holds the World Together

The Goddess falls in love with Herself, drawing forth her own emanation, which takes on a life of its own. Love of self for self is the creative force of the universe. Desire is the primal energy, and that energy is erotic: the attraction of lover to beloved, of planet to star, the lust of electron for proton. Love is the glue that holds the world together.

—**Starhawk, in** *The Spiral Dance: A Rebirth of the Ancient Religions of the Great Goddess*

45

Respect Yourself

Learn to be alone
without being lonely.
Learn to admire your beauty
without finding fault.
Learn to love yourself
without the love of others.

—**h.r.d.**

46

Life Comes at You Fast

This life you must know
as the tiny splash of a raindrop:
A thing of beauty that disappears as it comes into being.
Therefore, set your goal.

—Buddhist Prayer

47

Listen to the Wisdom of Your Own Heart

Turn within and seek the wisdom of your higher self. It is able to
speak to us from the combined wisdom of our heart, mind, and spirit.

—Madisyn Taylor

48

Today Is the First Day of the Rest of Your Life

This is the beginning of a new day.
I can waste it or use it for good.
What I do today is important because I am exchanging a day of my
life for it.
When tomorrow comes, this day will be gone forever,
leaving in its place something for which I have traded it.
I want it to be a gain, not a loss;
good, not evil;
success, not failure—
in order that I shall not regret the price I paid for it today.

—Unknown

49

Cover Our Earth with Flowers

Cover my earth mother four times with many flowers.
Let the heavens be covered with the banked-up clouds.
Let the earth be covered with fog;
cover the earth with rains.
Great waters, rains, cover the earth.
Lightning cover the earth.
Let thunder be heard over the earth;
let thunder be heard;
Let thunder be heard over the six regions of the earth.

—Native American Chant

50

Love and Miracles

Let me always insist on miracles to
celebrate love.
And when all I love on earth
lies lifeless in my arms
let me offer it to you with such freedom of heart
That I am swept up into the heavens. Amen.

—Mary Lou Kownacki

51

Water Is Life

We travel your powerful currents
to meet our relations.
We flood our rice fields.
We bathe our children.
We cleanse the dead.
We baptize, we purify, we do ablutions,
We immerse in the mikvah.
We heal with you—Holy Water.
We remember to protect you.

—Water Protection Women

52

A Message to Take to God

Saint Therese, the little flower,
Please pick me,
A rose from the heavenly garden,
And send it to me
With a message of love.
Ask God to grant me
The favor I thee implore
And tell him I will love him
Each day more and more.

—Prayer of Petition to St. Thérèse of Lisieux

53
Believe in the Human Spirit

We pray for an end to cruelty,
whether to humans or other animals,
for an end to bullying, and torture in all its forms.
We pray that we may learn the peace that comes with forgiving
and the strength we gain in loving;
that we may learn to take nothing for granted in this life;
that we may learn to see and understand with our hearts;
that we may learn to rejoice in our being.
We pray for these things with humility;
We pray because of the hope that is within us,
and because of a faith in the ultimate triumph of the human spirit;
We pray because of our love for Creation, and because of our trust
in God.
We pray, above all, for peace throughout the world.

—Dr. Jane Goodall

54
We Are All One

We light the light of a new idea.
It is the light of our coming together.
It is the light of our growing;
to know new things,
to see new beauty,
to feel new love.

—Unitarian Invocation

55

Truth, Life, and Love

Thy kingdom come.
Let the reign of divine Truth, Life, and Love
be established in me, and
rule out of me all sin;
and may Thy Word enrich
the affections of all mankind,
and govern them!

—Mary Baker Eddy

56

Maiden Mother Crone

Hold thy shield over us, protect us all.
Danu beloved! Mother of the Shining Ones,
Shield, oh shield us, Lady of nobleness,
And Brigit the beauteous, shepherdess of the flocks,
Safeguard thou our animals, encircle us together,
O Mother! O Maiden! O Crone of Wisdom!

—Ancient Celtic Oral Tradition

57

On Earth as It Is in Heaven

Our Father which art in heaven,
Hallowed be thy name.
Thy kingdom come.

Thy will be done, on earth
as it is in heaven.
Give us this day our daily bread.
And forgive us our trespasses,
as we forgive those
who trespass against us.
And lead us not into temptation,
but deliver us from evil:
For thine is the kingdom,
and the power, and the glory,
forever and ever.
Amen.

—Matthew 6:9–13

58
The Ancient Wisdom of Women

Our old women gods, we ask you!
Our old women gods, we ask you!
Then give us long life together,
May we live until our frosted hair is white;
May we live till then.
This life that now we know!

—Tewa Traditional Prayer

59

Learning the Art of Forgiveness

Our Father, Holy Mother,
Creator of the Cosmos, Source of Life,
You are in my mind, in my garden,
in my cup of wine and loaf of bread.
May we give each other strength, mercy,
tenderness, and joy
and forgive each other's failures,
silence, pettiness, and forgetfulness
as we ask to be forgiven
by those we've hurt.
Lead us home
to ourselves, to You,
to clarity, to oneness
and deliver us from the darkness
of our ignorance and fear.
So we pray and so we receive. Amen.

—Jan Phillips

60

There Are Blessings Everywhere

Blessed is the spot,
and the house,
and the place,
and the city,
and the heart,
and the mountain,
and the refuge,
and the cave,
and the valley,
and the land,
and the sea,
and the island,
and the meadow
where mention of God hath been made
and His praise glorified.

—Anonymous

Prayer Practice: Rites of Passage

Ceremonies celebrating rites of passage are used in many religions and cultures in different ways and are celebrated at different times of a person's life. Celebrations such as the Croning Ceremony for Wiccans and Na'ii'ees for the Apache have important significance in the lives of women and girls and focus on celebrating womanhood and feminine power. At the core of these celebrations is reflection on the past, wisdom, and growth, and many rites of passage for women are particularly used to connect to other women as well. In theory, the concept of a rite of passage does not have to be a literal celebration or have religious significance like most practices but can be a reflection upon blessings, a prayer for growth, or something to commemorate the passing of a threshold.

What the World Needs Now: LOVE

"You don't have to be anything but yourself to be worthy."

—Tarana Burke

"You know, you do need mentors, but in the end, you really just need to believe in yourself."

—Diana Ross

"When we step up for ourselves, we create opportunity."

—Kerry Washington

"Every day is a great day to feel good about yourself. Feeling good makes you look good—that's my motto."

—Katie Meade

"You can't eat beauty, it doesn't sustain you. What is fundamentally beautiful is compassion for yourself and those around you. That kind of beauty inflames the heart and enchants the soul."

—Lupita Nyong'o

Chapter Three

March:
Women Making a Difference

"Each time a woman stands up for herself, without knowing it, possibly without claiming it, she stands up for all women."

—Maya Angelou

"I do not wish women to have power over men, but over themselves."

—Mary Shelley

"There is no limit to what we as women can accomplish."

—Michelle Obama

"It seems to me that I cannot afford, as a self-respecting individual, to refuse to do a thing merely because it will make me disliked or bring down a storm of criticism on my head."

—Eleanor Roosevelt

"You are enough. You are so enough. It is unbelievable how enough you are."

—Sierra Boggess

"Don't complain about what you don't have. Use what you've got. To be less than your best is a sin."

—Oprah Winfrey

61

For All Women through the Ages

Spirit of the realm, God of many names, and one transforming and abundant love, we turn this month in our nation's life to reflect on the stories, the heritage, and the struggles of women throughout the ages. We seek to learn from all those voices that have been left unheard. May we pause before the silences of the ages, find who has been left out, and craft new ways of inclusion for every week and every month. May this spiritual practice bring out the voices of all those struggling, all those left apart. May we let go of our assumptions and cold comforts [and] of what is the normal to live by, unless it be a standard that is rooted in compassion, in inclusivity, in diversity. May this month of reflection teach us to search for those stories that are different from our own.

—Revered Jude Geiger

62

We Are All Reborn

It's okay
if you're burning
with anger
or sadness
or both
it is necessary
for you to collapse
so you can learn
how phoenixes are reborn
when they burn

and rise again
from the ashes of
their existence

—Noor Unnahar

63
My Wish for You

Whatever you choose, however many roads you travel, I hope that you choose not to be a lady. I hope you will find some way to break the rules and make a little trouble out there. And I also hope that you will choose to make some of that trouble on behalf of women.

—Nora Ephron

64
Keep Holding On

Hold on to what is good
even if it is
a handful of earth.
Hold on to what you believe
even if it is
a tree which stands by itself.
Hold on to what you must do
even if it is
a long way from here.
Hold on to life even when
it is easier letting go.

Hold on to my hand even when
I have gone away from you.

—Nancy Wood

65

Courage Takes Many Forms

Courage does not always roar.
Sometimes courage is the quiet voice
at the end of the day saying, "I will try again tomorrow."

—Mary Anne Radmacher

66

May We Walk Where the Grass Is Green

Oh our Mother the Earth,
Oh our Father the Sky,
Your children are we, and with tired backs
We bring you the gifts that you love.
Then weave for us a garment of brightness.
May the warp be the bright light of morning;
May the fringes be the falling rain;
May the borders be the standing rainbow.
Thus weave for us a garment of brightness,
that we may walk fittingly where birds sing;
That we may walk fittingly where grass is green.
Oh our Mother the Earth, oh our Father the Sky.

—Tewa Tribal Song

67
O Mother of the World

Remember, O most gracious Virgin Mary,
that never was it known that
anyone who fled to your protection,
implored your help,
or sought your intercession,
was left unaided.

—Memorare, Roman Catholic Prayer

68
May Peace Be with Us Always

Praise ye, Ngai… Peace be with us.
Say that the elders may have wisdom and speak with one voice.
Peace be with us.
Say that the country may have tranquility.
Peace be with us.
And the people may continue to increase.
Peace be with us.
Say that the people and the flock and the herds
May prosper and be free from illness.
Peace be with us.
Say that the fields may bear much fruit
And the land may continue to be fertile.
Peace be with us.
May peace reign over earth,
May the gourd cup agree with [the] vessel.
Peace be with us.

May their heads agree and every ill word be driven out
Into the wilderness, into the virgin forest.
Praise ye, Ngai… Peace be with us.

—Kikuyu, Kenyan Chant

69
Silent Prayer

Pray inwardly, even if you do not enjoy it.
It does good, though you feel nothing.
Yes, even though you think you are doing nothing.

—Julian of Norwich, 1373

70
A Prayer to St. Joan of Arc, for Faith

In the face of your enemies, in the face of harassment, ridicule, and doubt, you held firm in your faith. Even in your abandonment, alone and without friends, you held firm in your faith. Even as you faced your own mortality, you held firm in your faith. I pray that I may be as bold in my beliefs as you, St. Joan. I ask that you ride alongside me in my own battles. Help me be mindful that what is worthwhile can be won when I persist. Help me hold firm in my faith. Help me believe in my ability to act well and wisely. Amen.

—Anonymous

71
Let Me Walk in Beauty

Oh, Great Spirit,
whose voice I hear in the winds
and whose breath gives life to all the world, hear me.
I am small and weak.
I need your strength and wisdom.
Let me walk in beauty and make my eyes
ever behold the red and purple sunset.
Make my hands respect the things you have made
and my ears sharp to hear your voice.
Make me wise so that I may understand
the things you have taught my people.
Let me learn the lessons you have hidden
in every leaf and rock.

—Lakota Chant

72
May Everybody Be Happy!

Oh Almighty! May he protect all of us!
May he cause us to enjoy!
May we acquire strength together.
May our knowledge become brilliant!
May we not hate each other!
Oh Almighty! May there be a Peace! Peace!! Peace!!! Everywhere.
Oh Almighty! May everybody be happy!
May all be free from ailments!
May we see what is auspicious!

May no one be subject to miseries!
Oh Almighty! May there be a Peace! Peace! Peace! Everywhere.

—Indian Song, 1400 BC

Prayer Practice: Meditation

Meditation is one of the most universal spiritual practices, and some form of it is used in almost every religion worldwide. It has been proven to stabilize your mood, ease pain, and even make women smarter. While some forms of meditation are more strict, even the simplest forms of meditation can help you become more connected to yourself and your spirituality. Taking a moment to contemplate in silence, pray, or let your mind go blank in a quiet space or using objects that hold personal significance can help you reach a deeper understanding of yourself or assist you through difficulties. Meditation is a very versatile tactic that can be combined with many other practices to make your prayer more meaningful.

73

A Prayer for Women Leaders around the World

Praise to you, women leaders of the seven continents, for your many
works of justice.
Praise to you, women leaders of Asia, for confronting trafficking
of women.
Praise to you, women leaders of Africa, for raising your voices to
stop AIDS.
Praise to you, women leaders of Europe, for your peacekeeping.
Praise to you, women leaders of North America,
for confronting economic inequities and racism.
Praise to you, women leaders of South America,
for struggling against US domination of your land.
Praise to you, women leaders in Antarctica,
for your scientific research.
Praise to you, women leaders of Australia, for supporting
indigenous cultures.

—Diann Neu

74

If Not Now: A Prayer for Women

Who will stand now, if not for me?
Who will rise now and march now and sing a song
of freedom's call now? Who, if not for me?
Once more, and yet again, if not now, when?

—Stacey Zisook Robinson

75

Freedom

So free am I, so gloriously free
Free from three petty things—
From mortar, from pestle, and from my twisted lord,
Freed from rebirth and death I am,
And all that has held me down is hurled away.

—Mutta, Sixth Century Buddhist Poet

76

Women of Colour

our backs
tell stories
no books have
the spine to
carry

—rupi kaur

77

Seek the Light

The Sun, the Light of the world,
I hear Him coming.
I see his face as He comes.
He makes the beings on earth happy.
And they rejoice.
O Wakan-Tanka, I offer to You this world of Light.

—Sioux Song

78
The Wisdom of Deep Listening

Our Aboriginal culture has taught us to be still and to wait.
We do not try to hurry things up.
We let them follow their natural course—like the seasons.
We watch the moon in each of its phases.
We wait for the rain to fill our rivers and water the thirsty earth…
We wait on God, too.
His time is the right time.
We wait for him to make his Word clear to us.
We don't worry.
We know that in time and in the spirit of *dadirri*
(that deep listening and quiet stillness)
his way will be clear.

—**Miriam-Rose Ungunmerr-Baumann,
Aboriginal Artist & Teacher**

79
True Grace

Carry out a random act of kindness,
with no expectation of reward,
safe in the knowledge
that one day someone
might do the same for you.

—**Princess Diana**

80

Love and Friendship toward All Beings

O Lord! Make myself such that I may have love for all beings,
Joy in the meritorious, unstinted sympathy for the distressed,
And tolerance towards the perversely inclined.
O Lord! May my soul always find fulfillment, in friendship and love
towards all beings,
In all the virtuous, in compassion toward all suffering creatures,
And in remaining neutral towards those hostile to me.
This is my prayer.

—Ancient Jain Blessing

81

Life Is Not for the Faint of Heart

Fearlessness is better
than a faint heart
for any man who puts
his nose out of doors.
The length of my life and the day
of my death were fated long ago.

—Ancient Norse Verse

82

Prayer to Start the Day

O Infinite God, of life, goodness, and generous
love, I dedicate my heart, my life, to you.

Help me to cherish all human life
and do the good you want me to do.
Make me a loving example of your generous love
and a blessing to everyone I see.
May your goodness be fully in us, and in all that we
think and say and do.

—Unknown

83

May I Be a Living Sign of Your Generous Love

O God, may I find and praise your goodness
dwelling within every human being.
May I be a living sign of your generous love
and help everyone to live more intimately with you.
May we respect the evolving nature of all creation
and grow to our fullness of life with you.
Guide our search into our entire human nature, and
into all creation, to know what you want us to do.

—Unity Petition

84

Deeds, Words, and Wishes

O Goddess,
In my heart and spirit always,
May the blessed Maiden
And the Silver Bough of Faerie dwell,
Oh, in my heart and spirit always,

May the loving Maiden
And the tinkling Silver Bough of Faerie dwell.

—Ancient Irish Prayer

85

Let There Be No Injustice in Our World

O God, we pray for all those in our world
who are suffering from injustice:
For those who are discriminated against
because of their race, color, or religion;
For those imprisoned
for working for the relief of oppression;
For those who are hounded
for speaking the inconvenient truth;
For those tempted to violence
as a cry against overwhelming hardship;
For those deprived of reasonable health and education;
For those suffering from hunger and famine;
For those too weak to help themselves
who have no one else to help them;
For the unemployed who cry out
for work but do not find it.
We pray for anyone of our acquaintance
who is personally affected by injustice.
Forgive us, Lord, if we unwittingly share in the conditions
or in a system that perpetuates injustice.
Show us how we can serve your children
and make your love practical by washing their feet.

—Mother Teresa (St. Teresa of Calcutta)

86
Our Children Are Our Future and Hold All Our Hopes

O God! Educate these children.
These children are the plants of Thine orchard,
the flowers of Thy meadow,
the roses of Thy garden.
Let Thy rain fall upon them;
let the Sun of Reality shine upon them with Thy love.
Let Thy breeze refresh them in order
that they may be trained, grow, and develop,
and appear in the utmost beauty.
Thou art the Giver.
Thou art the Compassionate.

—Bahá'í Blessing

87
Compassion for All Including Ourselves

Help us not forget our Source,
Yet free us from not being in the Present.
From you arises every Vision, Power, and Song
from gathering to gathering.
Amen.

—Crane Dance Collective

88
Reach High

Every great dream begins with a dreamer.
Always remember, you have within you the strength, the patience,
and the passion to reach for the stars to change the world.

—Harriet Tubman

89
May This Beautiful World Never End

סלועל רמגי אלש ,ילא ,ילא
סיהו לוחה
סימה לש שורשר
סימשה קרב
סדאה תליפת

—

My God, My God, I pray that these things never end,
The sand and the sea,
The rustle of the waters,
Lightning of the Heavens,
The prayer of Man.

**—Hannah Szenes (aka Hannah Senesh), World War II
Resistance hero**

90

Take from My Heart All Anxiety

Take from my heart all painful anxiety;
let nothing sadden me but sin,
nothing delight me but the hope
of coming to the possession of You
my God and my all,
in your everlasting kingdom.
Amen.

—Suscipe of Catherine McAuley, 1778–1841

The Awesome Power of Women and Girls

"If one man can destroy everything, why can't one girl change it?"

—Malala Yousafzai

"Women are builders of civil society. We are the ones who are going to build it. You know why? We have no choice. Either you shut up, and you are humiliated, or you do what I'm doing. You scream."

—Fatema Mernissi

"If you want to have a life that is worth living, a life that expresses your deepest feelings and emotions and cares and dreams, you have to fight for it."

—Alice Walker

"You can be a thousand different women. It's your choice which one you want to be. It's about freedom and sovereignty. You celebrate who you are. You say, 'This is my kingdom.'"

—Salma Hayek

Chapter Four

April:
The Season of New Life

"I prayed to God to make me strong and able to fight, and that's what I've always prayed for ever since."

—Harriet Tubman, writing to Ednah Dow Cheney, 1865

"You just have to find your activism, and don't let anyone tell you what that should look like. If you're doing the work and you're getting someone to think, you're on the right path."

—Angie Thomas

"Think like a queen. A queen is not afraid to fail. Failure is another stepping-stone to greatness."

—Oprah Winfrey

"If adventures will not befall a young lady in her own village, she must seek them abroad."

—Jane Austen

"I think there is a feeling by some people in politics and in my own community that the woman can think she's leading all that she wants, have a semblance of influence, but the ultimate voice rests with the man....I am not one who subscribes to that."

—Ilhan Omar

91

New Growth

A single act of kindness throws out roots in all directions,
and the roots spring up and make new trees.
The greatest work that kindness does to others is that it makes them
kind themselves.

—Amelia Earhart

92

May We Always Be Kind as an Example to Our Children

May we learn contentment and satisfaction.
May we learn to enjoy contentment,
which brings great freedom into our lives
and brings us so much happiness.
May we be an example to the world.

—Buddhist Prayer

93

Daughters Become Mothers

May it be Your wish, G-d our Lord and G-d of our ancestors,
Ruler of mercy: that the same way
You have saved me from this great pain and from the dangers of
giving birth,
so too may Your mercies pour forth
to rescue all the daughters of Abraham, Isaac, and Jacob,

the descendants of those who truly loved You, from this danger.
As You have saved me now,
so do I beg You to show me a sign of favor
each time that I give birth. Amen.

—Ancient Hebrew Song

94

Let Us Be Love in Action

May we be the transformation we wish to see in the world.
From the inside out…
From the roots branching upwards…
From the heart
to thought
to word
to action.
Through life's trials and hardships
we can arise beautiful and free.

—Julia Butterfly Hill

95

Prayer for a Healthy Pregnancy

Dear God,
May you watch my sleep as I carry this baby.
May your hand be upon this little life as it develops in my womb.
May you fill our hearts with joy, and our bodies with peace.
May we feel you so close to us as we sense your amazing creativity
at work.

We rest in you.
Amen.

—Morning Star Women's Group

96

Blessings with Every Step You Take

May the road rise up to meet you.
May the wind be always at your back.
May the sun shine warm upon your face;
the rains fall soft upon your fields, and until we meet again,
May God hold you in the palm of His hand.

—Irish Blessing

97

A Guide for Those Who Lost Their Way

May I become at all times, both now and forever
A protector for those without protection
A guide for those who have lost their way
A ship for those with oceans to cross
A bridge for those with rivers to cross
A sanctuary for those in danger
A lamp for those without light
A place of refuge for those who lack shelter
And a servant to all in need.

—Buddhist Chant

98
Peace in Every Step

God be between you and harm in
all the empty places you walk.

—Egyptian Blessing, 1729

99
A World Yet Undreamed

We can create a world as yet unimagined, a world undreamed, yet
dimly felt. We are like the corn. Mysteriously hidden within each of us
are the seeds that can germinate into a new society, a new planet. Like
the corn, we have hidden deep within our living process a wisdom
that reaches back to all knowledge and beyond to all possibilities. Our
very existence is potential. Potential is always that which is, as yet,
unexpressed. We have the wisdom of the ancestors reaching back to
the mighty power of all creation…within us.

—Anne Wilson Schaef

100
Hold to Hope

Hope is the thing with feathers
that perches in the soul
and sings the tunes
without the words and never stops at all.

—Emily Dickinson

101
God Is within Me and God Is All around Me

May all I say and all I think
be in harmony with Thee,
God within me, God beyond me,
Maker of the Trees.

—Chinook Prayer

102
Prayer for an Easy Pregnancy

May it be your will, God, my Lord and the Lord of my ancestors,
that You will ease for me the difficulty of pregnancy,
and that You will increase my strength and the strength of my
unborn baby
When my time to give birth will arrive, I will give birth easily
and without any pain, and the baby will go out into the air of the
world easily,
without any harm to me or to the baby.
And the baby will be born with good luck [mazal tov], into life, peace,
health, wealth, and honor,
and will find grace in Your eyes and in the eyes of all your creations.

—Hebrew Prayer

Prayer Practice: New Beginnings

Many types of new beginnings, like births and weddings, are celebrated regularly, but blessing other beginnings can make crossing thresholds even more meaningful. Getting a group of friends together to have a meal, share stories, or read poems or scripture can be the perfect way to celebrate a new job, a baby's first steps, or moving to a new city. In India, family and friends gather for housewarming celebrations: a fire is lit, Puja is performed, and the empty house is blessed by the gods and loved ones. Having those close to you share their wishes and prayers for your new beginning will help you and bless you as you celebrate this change.

103
The Soul of the World

The inhabitant or soul of the universe is never seen;
its voice alone is heard…
It has a gentle voice like a woman,
a voice so fine and gentle
that even children cannot become afraid.
What it says is, "Be not afraid of the universe."

—Inuit Proverb

104
To Be Made New

Today I hold still
To balance and recharge,
To release the day before
And prepare for the day ahead.
I thank You for this opportunity
to be made new.

—Abigail Wurdeman

105
We Are One

Justice rolls down like a river
Compassion and peace shall flow like a stream,
The hills, rocks and valleys, oceans and trees

Sing out their song: We are one.
Sing out their song: We are one.

—Diane Forrest, OP

106

Every Child Is a New Promise: Prayer for a Pregnant Woman

Father, I carry within me
New promise.
I cherish the very breath of creation within me
Stirring within my womb, growing and changing each day.
We sleep with peace,
We sing with the angels
And rest in you always. Amen.

—Anonymous

107

How to Not Block the Blessings

There's a reason the sun rises anew each day.
Every day is a completely clean slate.
Cherry-picking bad memories
and rolling them around in my head all day,
it's hard to remember that
I've been blessed with forgiveness.
Forever. For good.
Somehow I seem to think
I've got to make amends in perpetuity,

that I need to keep re-living my mistakes
till it blocks the blessings from coming in.
But happiness is really just a habit;
a decision to accept grace and embrace joy.
Make me a work in progress
who actually acknowledges the progress I've made
and the work we've done together.

—Ruth Williams

108

Harness

Little soul,
you and I will become
the memory
of a memory of a memory.
A horse
released of the traces
forgets the weight of the wagon.

—Jane Hirshfield

109

Be a Candle in the Dark

Each day can't be a good day.
But within each day—those
long twenty-four hours—there
are a few minutes or even
seconds when something good

or special happens.
Those moments are as powerful
As the frail flame of a candle
That can light an entire dark room.

—Judith Garrett Garrison and Scott Sheperd

110
There Is a Sacred Happiness for Us All

May all beings have happiness and the causes of happiness;
May all be free from sorrow and the causes of sorrow;
May all never be separated from the sacred happiness which
is sorrowless;
And may all live in equanimity, without too much attachment and too
much aversion,
And live believing in the equality of all that lives.

—Buddhist Chant

111
Grow in Love

Help us to do the things we should,
to be to others kind and good;
in all we do, in work or play,
to grow more loving every day.

—Rebecca Weston, 1890

112
Birthing Blessings

Help me to protect and nurture and guide
this new yet undiscovered soul.
And let me not curse the child or myself
when we both prove to be only human.

—Merle Feld

113
Mother and Child in Your Safe Arms

Come lay your gentle hand upon us as we draw near to the birth.
Fill our hearts with excitement;
Cover our lives with hope.
Guide us through labor
Into a new season.
I give you both my joys and fears
And choose to put my trust in you.
I trust in you to shelter us both,
Mother and child, within your safe arms.
Amen.

—Mothers Prayer Circle of Agape

114
Prayer for All Babies

We pray Your loving protection over all babies and their families
and pray that many may be brought up to know the Lord Jesus as
their Savior.
We pray for parents and grandparents and all those that are in any
way connected
with young babies to have the wisdom and grace to care for them
in a loving and secure environment. Guard and protect,
guide and provide for each innocent little baby.
This we ask in Jesus' name, Amen.

—Big Island Sunday School

115
God Is with Us Always

In the beginning was God,
Today is God,
Tomorrow will be God.
Who can make an image of God?
He has no body.
He is the word which comes out of your mouth.
That word!
It is no more,
It is past, and still it lives!
So is God.

—African Prayer

116

Appeal to the Great Mother

Lady, weave your web of change
Bring the world to peace again
Let us all be kin together
So Mote It Be.

—Rowan Fairchild

117

When I Lay Me Down to Sleep

Keep far from me at night
All things that me affright
And wake me safe with sunshine bright
within my heart;
If not within my sight.

—Doris Howe

118

In Perfect Peace: Prayer for Babies to Sleep

Father, You have said in Scripture that You give
Your beloved sleep
and I ask that You would bless our beloved little baby
with a deep, refreshing, and uninterrupted night's sleep.

—Parish Prayer

Chapter Five

May:
The Greatest Thing and the
Hardest Thing

"Live your life while you have it. Life is a splendid gift. There is nothing small in it. For the greatest things grow by God's law out of the smallest. But to live your life, you must discipline it."

—Florence Nightingale

"In life there are journeys in which you must go.
sometimes the road is just unknown
but trust you must your path is right
even though there appears no end in sight.
The day you take that leap of faith
is the day you step toward your blessed fate."

—Jasmeine Moonsong

"Today is the day to break free from the prison of the person you know yourself to be and step into a self you have yet to know. Will it be comfortable? No, but do it anyway."

—Debbie Ford

"What you are now is the result of what you were. What you will be tomorrow will be the result of what you are now."

—Henepo Gunarata

"A mother's arms are made of tenderness and children sleep soundly in them."

—Victor Hugo

119

Give Me Grace This Day and Every Day

Lord, please fill me with your grace so that I may be restored and renewed in my role as a mother. Help me to remember that I do not have to do this alone—that you are with me to strengthen and guide me.

—Theresa Collier

120

Listen to the Wisdom of Women

Listen, my son, to your father's instruction and do not forsake your mother's teaching. They are a garland to grace your head and a chain to adorn your neck.

—Proverbs 1:8–9

121

Like a Bridge Over Troubled Water

When trouble is close at hand.
Your Word will be a lamp for me,
a guide to light my way,
a solid place to set my feet,
a compass when I stray.

—Mary Fairchild

122
Mom's Prayer

Dear Lord, it's such a hectic day,
With little time to stop and pray,
For life's been anything but calm
Since you called me to be a Mom.
Yet, when I steal a moment, Lord,
Just at the sink or ironing board,
To ask the blessings of Your grace,
I see then in my small one's face,
That you have blessed me all the while
And I stoop to kiss that precious smile.

—Anonymous

123
The Wisdom of Our Grandmothers

Dear Lord, bless every mother and every grandmother
with the finest of your spiritual blessings today.
Validate her worth daily so she has no reason to doubt
whether she is loved, valued, and cherished
in the eyes of her Heavenly Father.
Create in her a deep sense of your protection and trust,
so that worry and fear will disappear as she places
her loved ones into Your care. Let her know that
every prayer she has prayed and every encouraging word
she has spoken on behalf of her children/grandchildren

has been transformed into sweet, fragrant offerings before
Your throne.

—Rebecca Barlow Jordan

124

An Angel to Protect You: Irish Prayer for a Newborn

May strong arms hold you
Caring hearts tend you
And may love await you at every step.
May you bring light to the home
Warmth to the heart
Joy to the soul
And love to the lives you touch.
May God surround this child
And bless this day.
May you have a sunbeam to warm you
Good luck to charm you
An angel to protect you
Laughter to cheer you
And faithful friends near you.
May God hold you
In the hollow of his hand
Forever and ever.

—Celtic Blessing

125
Prayer for Motherhood

Draw close to all mothers, we pray, and guide and direct them as they carry out the roles and responsibilities of motherhood and draw them into close loving fellowship with their families and with You—this we ask in Jesus' name, Amen.

—Moms Circle of Springfield

126
Hope

On Sundays, the preacher gives everyone a chance
to repent their sins. Miss Edna makes me go
to church. She wears a bright hat;
I wear my suit. Babies dress in lace.
Girls my age, some pretty, some not so
pretty. Old ladies and men nodding.
Miss Edna every now and then throwing her hand
in the air. Saying *Yes, Lord* and *Preach!*
I sneak a pen from my back pocket,
bend down low like I dropped something.
The chorus marches up behind the preacher
clapping and humming and getting ready to sing.
I write the word HOPE on my hand.

—Jacqueline Woodson

127

The Compassionate Heart

If you're going to care
about the fall of the sparrow
you can't pick and choose
who's going to be the sparrow.
It's everybody.

—Madeleine L'Engle

128

A Prayer for Those Hurting

We pray for those who grieve today. We ask for your comfort to
surround those who weep. We pray for the peace of your presence
to cover our minds and thoughts; as you remind us, the enemy can
never steal us out of your hands. We lay it all down at your feet, every
burden, every care, believing that is the safest place for it to be. We
love you, Lord, we need your fresh grace. In the Powerful Name of
Jesus, Amen.

—Debbie McDaniel

129

For Single Moms Who Do So Much for Us All

Father God, we thank you for each and every woman you have blessed
with the privilege of motherhood. We thank you that each single
mother is a Godly steward of each of their children and that they
raise them in the ways of the Lord. Father, we pray and ask that You

continue to give them grace to walk the path of being a single parent with kindness and generosity. We pray that each single mother has a relationship with You and worships You in spirit and truth.

—Jennifer Maggis

130
Gratitude for My Mother

Dear Lord, today I turn to you to give you thanks for my mother. With your own gift of life, she bore me in her womb and gave me life. Please bless her, Lord, and comfort her. Most of all, Lord, on this Mother's Day, give my mother the graces she most needs and desires today. I ask you this, in the name of Jesus, our Lord and Savior forever and ever.

—Unknown

131
We Are Here to Love

You know well enough
that Our Lord does not look
so much at the greatness of our actions,
nor even at their difficulty,
but at the love with which we do them.

—St. Thérèse de Lisieux, "The Little Flower"

132

In Support of Every Stressed-Out Mom

May you have clarity of thought and a morsel of sanity today. May you know that His grace is enough. For every season, every tantrum, every question, every failure, it is enough—always. He adores you, just because. And with of this knowledge, may you feel empowered to love your children the same way: the way God asks you to, the way your kids deserve, and the way you want to love them. May your dreams be sweet and your sleep be restful. Sleep well, Momma, knowing that the work you are doing is good, and your Father is smiling on you.

—Malinda Fuller

133

Working Mothers Are Our Heroes

My Loving Creator,
You know how really tired I am.
On days when things are really frantic,
I consider how you made the world in seven days—
and then I try to remember that you aren't asking me to recreate that feat.
Please help me to remain a loving mother to my children
and to keep some balance in my life.
Most of all, my caring Father,
let me remember to ask for help and to rely on you for strength
when I have none left; for patience when mine is so often gone;
and for the wisdom and endless well of compassion
and love I need in my job as mother.

—Unity Church San Francisco

134
Lay Down Your Burden of Worry

Lord, I trust in you and lean on you. I thank you for your mercy and provision for me and my family. I come to you again and ask that your will be done in this situation we are currently facing. Guard my heart and my mind and keep me focused on your will. Lord, please send your Holy Spirit to breathe your peace into my soul and walk with me on this journey.

—Theresa Ceniccola

135
Take Time to Heal

To everything there is a season,
a time for every purpose under the sun.

—Ecclesiastes 3:1

136
Consolation, Comfort, and Calm

The love of God shines in me
and eternally sustains me

—Magdolene Mogyorosi

137
Let Every Voice Be Heard

May those without voice be heard.
May those without food be fed.
May those who are harmed be healed.
May the earth's health be restored.
May all have peace, equality, inclusion for all.

—Alycia Longriver Davis

138
God, Please Help My Adult Children

Father of Love, help my kids grow
in gratitude to you. Help me to affirm them and support them
with love,
that they might recognize authentic faith and love
and turn to you in their time of need.
Thank you, Lord. Thank you.

—Dallas Divinity

139
Fill Me with Strength and Restore My Spirit

Heavenly Father,
I come to you today, humble and exhausted,
and ask that you carry my burdens.
Lord, pour your heavenly nourishment

into my soul and give me the energy
to sustain me in my role as a mother.

—Theresa Ceniccola

140
The Gift of the Unexpected

You will not grow
if you sit in a beautiful flower garden,
but you will grow if you are sick,
if you are in pain,
if you experience losses,
and if you do not
put your head in the sand,
but take the pain and
learn to accept it,
not as a curse or punishment
but as a gift to you
with a very, very specific purpose.

—Elisabeth Kübler-Ross

141
Teach Me to Remember Kindness

Earth, teach me stillness as the grasses are stilled with light.
Earth, teach me suffering as old stones suffer with memory.
Earth, teach me humility as blossoms are humble with beginning.
Earth, teach me caring as the mother who secures her young.
Earth, teach me courage as the tree which stands all alone.

Earth, teach me limitation as the ant which crawls on the ground.
Earth, teach me freedom as the eagle which soars in the sky.
Earth, teach me resignation as the leaves which die in the fall.
Earth, teach me regeneration as the seed which rises in the spring.
Earth, teach me to forget myself as melted snow forgets its life.
Earth, teach me to remember kindness as dry fields weep with rain.

—Ute Nation of North America

142

We All Make Mistakes Sometimes

Heal the pain I carry in my heart each day and
close the distance between my children and me.
I ask this in the name of your most loving mother,
the mother of us all. Amen.

—Morning Star Church

143

The Empty Nest

Remember not the events of the past, the things of long ago consider
not; see, I am doing something new! Now it springs forth, do you not
perceive it?

—Isaiah 43:18–19

144
A New Phase

Loving Spirit, what is this new thing you are doing in me? Help me to see what you have in store for me now. You are doing something new in me. You are preparing me for a new phase, a new service, and a new way of loving you. Keep my eyes clear and my heart open to the ways you call me, Lord. And help me always to be grateful for the many gifts of each day.

—Anonymous

Prayer Practice: Tkhines

Written in a time when most women could not read the established language of prayer books, Tkhines are personal prayers written for and by Jewish women for use every day and on special occasions. There are Tkhine prayers written for every significant event and for specific occasions in a woman's life, such as menarche, marriage, and maternity. Reciting the unique and personal prayers of their foremothers has helped many Jewish women feel more connected to their spirituality. The concept of these Tkhines can be used by any woman regardless of religion or culture; writing and reciting your own prayers for important moments in your life can help you through difficult times and bring you closer to your beliefs.

145
We Are All under the Same Sun

The sun shines down,
and its image reflects a thousand
different pots filled with water.
The reflections are many,

but they are each reflecting the same sun.
Similarly, when we come to know who we truly are,
we will see ourselves in all people.

—Amma

146

My Guide and My Refuge

O God!
Refresh and gladden my spirit.
Purify my heart.
Illumine my powers.

—Kimberly Lynn Davis

147

Enter into the Soul-Light

Step into the Sunlight
Feel the pain wash away
Enter in the Soul-light
Just BE in today.
Forget all emotion
Put your trust in the day
Let the past rush on by you
Put your Self in THE WAY.

—Lynne Milum

148

Lay Down Your Cares and Greet Life Open-Armed

Forget this world, forget this course, and come
with wholly empty hands unto your God.

—A Course in Miracles

149

Enlightenment Is for Everybody

Sentient beings are numberless,
I vow to free them.
Delusions are inexhaustible,
I vow to end them.
The Dharma Gates are boundless,
I vow to open them.
The Enlightened Way is unsurpassable,
I vow to embody it.

—Zen Teaching

150

Do Not Be Afraid

I say to you
you are like
the most beautiful and gentle clay
forming and shaping
as the breakers brush against the cliff
always moving

Wave that never ceases
you are one with the ocean's
altering horizons
where darkness meets light
and seasons shift
between our souls
let every breath
fill your mind with peace
let your soul unfold courageously
in divine wisdom
and open itself for the beautiful things
that want to enter your life from the future
the greatest truth of love
the only thing that matters
is that you are alive

—Samma Himmel

151

No Matter What, Never Stop

If you hear the dogs,
keep on going.
If you hear gunfire,
keep on going.
If you hear shouts and footsteps,
keep on going.

—Harriet Tubman

152

Sweet Mercy

My soul is weary.
Worry, fear, and doubt
Surround me,
On every side.
Yet your sweet mercy
Cannot be held back
From those that cry out to you.
Hear my cry.
Let me trust in your mercy.
Show me how.
Free me.
Free me from anxiety and stress
That I may find rest
In your loving arms.
Amen.

—Anonymous

Staying on the Path of Hope

"As long as you are responsible for building a healthy community, then that's what gives you motivation and hope, and prevents you from losing hope."

—Daisy Khan

"With nature's help, humankind can set into creation all that is necessary and life-sustaining."

—Hildegard of Bingen

"The heart is always the place to go. Go home into your heart, where there is warmth, appreciation, gratitude, and contentment."

—Ayya Khema

"A flower unfolds to the best of its ability due to the conditions around it. And so do you—you unfold to the best of your ability."

—Kuan Yin

Chapter Six

June:
Keep Moving Forward

"You can fall, but you can rise also."

—Angelique Kidjo

"Keep your face to the sunshine and you cannot see a shadow."

—Helen Keller

"Arrange whatever pieces come your way."

—Virginia Woolf

"Don't wait around for other people to be happy for you. Any happiness you get you've got to make yourself."

—Alice Walker

"A gracious woman gains respect."

—Proverbs 11:16

153
Do Not Despair

Let no sadness come to this heart.
Let not trouble come to these arms.
Let no conflict come to these eyes.
Let my soul be filled with the blessing of joy and peace.

—Hamsa Prayer

154
No Matter What, Forgive

We forget so easily, don't we?
Life on earth can be so painful.
In our lives that are just as short as they are long,
Just as precious as they are strong,
Please help us to remember.
That you love us all.

—Sister Bree

155
Safe and Secure in the Night

Father-Mother God,
Loving me—
Guard me when I sleep;
Guide my little feet
Up to Thee.

—Mary Baker Eddy

156
The Great Plan for Our World

Let Light and Love and Power
restore the Plan on Earth.

—Alice Bailey

157
The Spiral of Sanctity

Fire of the Spirit,
life of the lives of creatures,
Spiral of sanctity,
Bond of all natures,
glow of charity,
lights of clarity,
taste of sweetness to the fallen,
be with us and hear us.

—Hildegard of Bingen

158
You Made It To Here!

A year ago,
you did not know today.
You did not know
how you'd make it here.
But you made it here.
By grade, you made it here.

—Morgan Harper Nichols

159

Song of the Flock of Stars in the Sky

Deep peace of the flowing air to you.
Deep peace of the quiet earth to you.
Deep peace of the shining stars to you.
Deep peace of the infinite peace to you.

—Fiona Macleod, 1895

160

Time beyond the End, beyond the Beginning

Divine Mother of all Beings
Great Goddess of Compassion and Mercy
May my heart be home to you
like your island in the sea.
May I feel your presence guiding me in fear and rage.
May the strength and balance of your grace-filled body be mine when
I need them,
And may I walk in your Bodhisattva Way with trust and gladness,
Beyond time, beyond the end, beyond the beginning.

—Prayer to Kuan Yin

161

Deliverance

Dear God,
Deliver me to my passion.
Deliver me to my brilliance.

Deliver me to my intelligence.
Deliver me to my depth.
Deliver me to my nobility.
Deliver me to my beauty.
Deliver me to my power to heal.
Deliver me to You.
Amen.

—Marianne Williamson

162
At the Breaking of the World, We Still Have Your Love

Dear Lord,
I may not see the sun and moon lose their light.
I may not witness rivers turn red, or stars fall from the sky.
Yet there are times when my world becomes unhinged
and the foundations of what I believe crack and dissolve.
Give me the grace to believe that Your power is at work
in the turmoil of my life.
Lead me to remember that Your power is greater than all evil,
and though the world may rock and sometimes break,
it will in time be transformed by Your Love.

—Unknown

163
Find Something Better in Your Future

A very wise man once told me that you can't look back— you just have to put the past behind you, and find something better in your future.

—Jodi Picoult

164
We Are All Strands in the Web of Life

Father, may they all be one,
as you and I are one.

—John 17:11, The Last Prayer of Jesus

165
Mother Teresa's Favorite Prayer

Dear Jesus, help us to spread your fragrance everywhere we go.
Flood our souls with your spirit and life.
Penetrate and possess our whole being so utterly
that our lives may only be a radiance of yours.
Shine through us, and be so in us
that every person we should come in contact with
may feel your presence in our soul.
Let them look up and see no longer us, but only Jesus.
Stay with us, and then we shall begin to shine as you shine;
so to shine as to be a light to others;
the light, Jesus, will be all from you.
None of it will be ours.

It will be you shining on others through us.
Let us thus praise you in the way you love best,
by shining on those around us.
Let us preach you without preaching:
not by words, but by our example,
by the catching force,
the sympathetic influence of what we do,
the evident fullness of the love our hearts bear for you.
Amen.

—Mother Teresa (St. Teresa of Calcutta)

Prayer Practice: Symbols and Tokens

Symbols, tokens, and gestures are used around the world in many prayer practices and daily rituals; they are often meant to strengthen or add significance, intention, or purpose to a prayer, blessing, or ritual. For example, Hindu women draw geometric designs near their doorsteps, Catholics cross themselves and use rosaries, and, in some cultures, giving a gift is similar to blessing someone. Whether your practice is secular or religious, adding material objects or gestures can help add meaning and intention to prayers or meditations of any kind. Wearing the jewelry of a loved one, keeping healing crystals in your pocket, or lighting a candle as you pray can help personalize and strengthen your spiritual intent.

166
Be Filled with Ease Today

May I be filled with loving kindness.
May I be well.
May I be peaceful and at ease.
May I be happy.

—Ancient Buddhist Chant

167

There Is a Comfort for Every Sorrow

The best remedy for those who are afraid, lonely, or unhappy is to go outside, somewhere where they can be quiet, alone with the heavens, nature, and God. Because only then does one feel that all is as it should be and that God wishes to see people happy, amidst the simple beauty of nature. As long as this exists, and it certainly always will, I know that then there will always be comfort for every sorrow, whatever the circumstances may be. And I firmly believe that nature brings solace in all troubles.

—Anne Frank

168

A Godly Woman

A woman of beauty
A woman of grace
A woman of excellence
Beholding God's face

She walks with the Lord
With integrity
Knowing her purpose
And destiny
No matter what happens
She walks in God's love
Reflecting the beauty
Of her Father above.

—M.S. Lowndes

169
Where the Path of Life Leads Us

Laughter isn't even the other side of tears.
It is tears turned inside out.
Truly the suffering is great, here on earth.
We blunder along, shredded by our mistakes,
bludgeoned by our faults.
Not having a clue where
the dark path leads us.
But on the whole,
we stumble along bravely,
don't you think?

—Alice Walker

170
To Be a Virtuous Woman

Father, help me to be a capable, intelligent, and virtuous woman—
faithful, diligent, generous, and spiritually strong. May the law of love
and kindness always be in my heart and on my lips. In Jesus' name,
Amen.

—Alisha Gratehouse

171
We Are All the Children of God

Blessed are the poor in spirit:
for theirs is the kingdom of heaven.
Blessed are they that mourn:
for they shall be comforted.

—The Beatitudes, Matthew 5:3–9

172
A Woman of Peace

Father, I trust in You
and keep my thoughts fixed on You
and Your promises.
And You will keep me in perfect peace.
I let Your peace rule in my heart.
I allow it to settle any questions that arise in my mind.
I wholeheartedly trust in You.
In Jesus' Name, Amen.

—Alisha Gratehouse

173

I Will Love You Gently

If I must worry about how
I will live in my old age
without wealth
I would be without health now
and how can I live to be
old?
If I must worry about how
I will live in my old age
without love
I would be without dreams now
and how can I go on living
another day?
Allow me to sit in the sun
and listen to the sky.
I will love you gently.

—Chungmi Kim

174

Prayer to a Guardian Angel

Angel of God,
my guardian dear,
to whom God's love commits me here,
ever this day
be at my side

to light and guard,
to rule and guide.

—Catholic Liturgy

175
Don't Look Back

Make it a rule of life never to regret
and never to look back.
Regret is an appalling waste of energy;
you can't build on it;
it's only good for wallowing in.

—Katherine Mansfield

176
Light Speed

Stay on the path if you're suffering
by taking the steps you need to take.
Hang on and hang in there, because it's now
that you're growing at light speed.
You're never going backward, only forward.

—Anonymous

177
Auspicious Wish

At this very moment, for the peoples and the nations of the earth,
May not even the names disease, war, famine, and suffering be heard.

Rather may their moral conduct, merit, wealth, and
prosperity increase,
and may good fortune and well-being always arise for them.

—Buddhist Prayer

178
Worrying Will Not Solve Your Problem

When you begin to worry,
go find something to do.
Get busy being a blessing to someone;
do something fruitful…
Above all else,
remember that worrying is totally useless.
Worrying will not solve your problem.

—Joyce Meyer

179
Miracles Do Happen

I am united with Source,
at one with all the most miraculous healing energies of Creation,
and limitless in Wisdom, Appreciation, and Peace.

—Susyn Reeve

Care of the Soul

"I define joy as a sustained sense of well-being and internal peace—a connection to what matters."

—Oprah Winfrey

"There are two ways of spreading light: to be the candle or the mirror that reflects it."

—Edith Wharton

"You don't always have to be doing something. You can just be, and that's plenty."

—Alice Walker

"Think of all the beauty still left around you and be happy."

—Anne Frank

"Men judge us by the success of our efforts. God looks at the efforts themselves."

—Charlotte Brontë

Chapter Seven

July:
She Has Overcome

"In the very deep darkness of this world, little pinpoints of light show up very brightly and can shine a long way."

—Tenzin Palmo

"Pain is inevitable, suffering is not."

—Henepola Gunaratana

"To gain that which is worth having, it may be necessary to lose everything else."

—Bernadette Devlin

"But when your situation is hopeless, all you can do is turn the world upside down, transform it according to your wishes, and create anew."

—Fatema Mernissi

180
The Gift of Crisis

Emotional discomfort,
when accepted,
rises, crests, and falls
in a series of waves.
Each wave
washes parts of us away
and deposits treasures
we never imagined.

—Martha Beck

181
Help Me to Love Myself

Holy Spirit, help me to see the beauty
that I am, without and within.
Help me to love myself, unconditionally, without judgment.
This day and always, help me to honor my body,
to love it unconditionally, and to be grateful for its service.
Amen.

—Carol Hansen Grey

182
Mend What Is Broken: A Prayer for Health

Heavenly Father, I call on you right now in a special way.
It is through your power that I was created.

Every breath I take,
every morning I wake,
and every moment of every hour,
I live under your power.
Father, I ask you now to touch me with that same power.
Fill me with the healing power of your spirit.
Cast out anything that should not be in me.
Mend what is broken.
And Father, restore me to full health
in mind and body so that I may serve you the rest of my life.
I ask this through Christ our Lord.
Amen.

—b. madaras

183
Fully Alive

I will not die an unlived life.
I will not live in fear
of falling or catching fire.
I choose to inhabit my days,
to allow my living to open me,
to make me less afraid,
more accessible,
to loosen my heart
until it becomes a wing,
a torch, a promise.
I choose to risk my significance;
to live so that which came to me as seed

goes to the next as blossom
and that which came to me as blossom,
goes on as fruit.

—Dawna Markova

184
Walk the Good Road to the Day of Quiet

There is no other one to pray to but you.
You yourself, everything that you see,
everything that has been made by you.
The star nations all over the universe you have finished.
The four quarters of the earth you have finished.
The day, and in that day, everything you have finished.
Grandfather, Great Spirit, lean close to the earth
that you may hear the voice I send.
You towards where the sun goes down, behold me;
Thunder Beings, behold me!
You where the White Giant lives in power, behold me!
You where the sun shines continually,
whence come the daybreak star and the day, behold me!
You where the summer lives, behold me!
You in the depths of the heavens, an eagle of power, behold!
And you, Mother Earth, the only Mother,
you who have shown mercy to your children.
Hear me, four quarters of the world—a relative I am!
Give me the strength to walk the soft earth, a relative to all that is!
Give me the eyes to see and the strength to understand,
that I may be like you.

With your power only can I face the winds.
and walk the good road to the day of quiet.
This is my prayer; hear me!
The voice I have sent is weak,
yet with earnestness I have sent it.
Hear me!
It is finished. Hetchetu aloh!

—Oglala Sioux, 1930

185
Spirit Woman's Song

I am a shooting star woman, says
I am a shooting star woman, says
I am a whirling woman of colors, says
I am a whirling woman of colors, says
I am a clean woman, says
I am a clean woman, says
I am a woman who whistles, says
I am a woman who looks into the insides of things, says
I am a woman who investigates, says
I am a woman wise in medicine, says
I am a mother woman, says
Holy Father, says
I am a woman wise in medicine, says
I bring my lord eagle, says
I bring my opossum, says
I bring my lord eagle, says
I bring my whirlwind of colors, says

Father in heaven, says
Saint Christ, says
Father scribe, says
I am a spirit woman, says
I am a woman of light, says
I am a woman of the day, says
I am a Book woman, says
Holy Father, says
I am a saint woman, says
I am a spirit woman, says

—**Maria Sabina, Mazatec Mesoamerican Indian, 1956**

186

Song of Spirit

I am the wind on the sea
I am the ocean wave
I am the sound of the billows
I am the seven-horned stag
I am the hawk on the cliff
I am the dewdrop in sunlight
I am the fairest of flowers
I am the raging boar
I am the salmon in the deep pool
I am the lake on the plain
I am the meaning of the poem
I am the point of the spear
I am the god that makes fire in the head
Who levels the mountain?

Who speaks the age of the moon?
Who has been where the sun sleeps?
Who, if not I?

—The Song of Amergin, Celtic Invocation

187

May We Always Be Ready for the Long Journey

O, our Mother the Earth, hear us
and give us support.
O Spirit of the East,
send us your Wisdom.
O Spirit of the South,
may we tread your path.
O Spirit of the West,
may we always be ready for the long journey.
O Spirit of the North, purify us
with your cleansing winds.

—Oglala Sioux Tribal Chant

188

The Soul of Nature That Gives Life to the Universe

Great Spirit, Divine One, Creator
who is heaven earth rock wind insect tree fox
human of every size shape color
Holy are your infinite names chanted sung whispered
shouted in every language, tongue.

—Claudia L'Amoreaux

189

Drop Love Bombs Everywhere

Poems

Hugs

Music

Photography

Movies

Kind words

Smiles

Meditation and prayer

Dance

Social activism

Websites

Blogs

Random acts of kindness

—The Spiritual Revolutionaries

190

Take Refuge in the Shelter of Your Wings

Hear my cry, O God;

listen to my prayer.

From the ends of the earth I call to you,

I call as my heart grows faint;

lead me to the rock that is higher than I.

For you have been my refuge,

a strong tower against the foe;

I long to dwell in your tent forever
and take refuge in the shelter of your wings.

—Psalm 61:1–4

191

May We Always Be Merciful

We ask, O God, for the grace
to be our best selves.
We ask for the vision
to be builders of the human community
rather than its destroyers.
We ask for the humility as a people
to understand the fears and hopes of other peoples.

—Sister Joan Chittister

192

Welcome Good

Let gratitude be the pillow upon which you kneel to
say your nightly prayer. And let faith be the bridge
you build to overcome evil and welcome good.

—Maya Angelou

193
Simple Wisdom

Act justly.
Love mercy.
Walk humbly.

—Micah 8:8

194
With a Pure Heart

Help us to love each person because
they are a human being and created in the image of God.
Let not our race, color, religion, or ethnicity be a dividing factor
but may we see each person as a uniquely created individual worthy of
our love.
Help us to stand against senseless violence and not support
anyone who would divide others for their own gain.
Make us true instruments of your peace.
In Jesus' Holy name we ask. Amen.

—Valerie Cullers

195
Prayer for the Weary, Broken, and Afraid

Benedict, when the storm rages
around me,
and I can hold on no more,
when the waves of fear engulf me

and I am weary,
battered and sore,
take me then and steer me
storm-tossed, broken and afraid,
into the arms of your safe harbor
safely home.

—Prayer to St. Benedict

196
A Time for Change

If you stay stuck for a period of time,
this is given unto you by your soul
to give you a resting place.
At this place, you judge it as stuck.
See it as transition.

—Kuan Yin

197
By Light Divine

I am the Soul.
I am the Light Divine.
I am Love.
I am Will.
I am Fixed Design.

—Alice Bailey

Prayer Practice: Prayer Journals

It is a scientifically proven fact that writing something out will help you to remember it better; try writing out your prayers to help you focus on them and strengthen your intentions toward your wishes. Keeping a physical list of your prayers in a journal could help you feel more in touch with your spirituality, as could looking back on the prayers that have been answered. If your approach to spirituality is more secular, keeping a dream journal, list of goals, or vision board can have the same effects and help you work toward and achieve your goals!

198
The Present Moment Prayer

O present moment, you belong to me, whole and entire.
I desire to use you as best I can.

—St. Faustina

199
A Call for Justice for the World

Admirable St. Dymphna, how just you were to all whom you encountered, and how careful you were to give every person his due, and more than he might desire or expect. By your power with God, please come to assist us to be just to all we meet, and even to be generous in giving everyone more than strict justice requires. Amen.

—Catholic Liturgy

200
No Amount of Anxiety Can Change Your Future

When thinking about life,
remember this:
no amount of guilt
can change the past
and no amount of anxiety
can change the future.

—Unknown

201
Move and Groove

When you pray,
move your feet.

—African Proverb

202
The Wisdom of Forgiving Others

Forgiveness is not always easy.
At times, it feels more painful
than the wound we suffered,
to forgive the one that inflicted it.
And yet, there is no peace without forgiveness.

—Marianne Williamson

203
The Virtue of Patience

Thank you for your life of perfect patience, lived in my place.
Give me strength today to reflect your patience to others. Amen.

—Mollie Schairer

204
Soar

When you are in trouble, you need to put all your energies into
thinking that there is a way out. Then, the bottom, the dark hole,
becomes just a springboard from which you can leap so high that your
head might hit a cloud.

—Fatema Mernissi

205

My Blessing Goes with You

When the storms of life are strong
When you're wounded, when you don't belong
When you no longer hear my song
My blessing goes with you

**—from Celtic Woman Song "The Blessing,"
by B. Graham and D. Downes**

206

To Help Just One Person

Sometimes I feel overwhelmed
but I try to work one day at a time.
If we just worry about the big picture,
we are powerless.
So my secret is to start right away doing
whatever little work I can do.
I try to give joy to one person in the morning,
and remove the suffering of one person in the afternoon.
That's enough.
When you see you can do that, you continue,
and you give two little joys,
and you remove two little sufferings,
then three, and then four.
If you and your friends do not despise the small work,
a million people will remove a lot of suffering.
That is the secret. Start right now.

—Chân Không

207

Every Day Is Sacred

With visible breath I am walking.
A voice I am sending as I walk.
In a sacred manner I am walking.
With visible tracks I am walking.
In a sacred manner I walk.

—**Native American Chant**

208

Everything Will Be Alright

I will breathe.
I will think of solutions.
I will not let my worry control me.
I will not let my stress level break me.
I will simply breathe.
And it will be okay.
Because I don't quit.

—**Shayne McClendon**

209

Comfort and Strengthen My Soul

Out of the depths, I cry to you, Lord!
My soul is overwhelmed with sorrow;
have mercy on me, according to your unfailing love.

May your Word of truth comfort and strengthen my soul.
Be my Light, my Strength, my Hope, and my Peace. Amen.

—Susan Glende

210

Novena to Mary, Queen of All Hearts

Mary, Queen of All Hearts,
Advocate of the most hopeless cases;
Mother most pure, most compassionate;
Mother of Divine Love,
full of divine light,
we confide to your care the favors
which we ask of you today.

—Catholic Liturgy

211

Come What May

Let come what comes, and accommodate yourself to that, whatever
it is. If good mental images arise, that is fine. If bad mental images
arise, that is fine, too. Look on all of it as equal, and make yourself
comfortable with whatever happens.

—Henepola Gunaratana

212
A Trusting Heart

You, God, are a mighty healer
and an ever-present help in trouble.
Help me to come to you with a trusting heart.
Please fill me with your peace.
May I find my hope and joy in you. Amen.

—Dawn Nichols

Women Get Stronger in the Face of Difficulty

"There are opportunities even in the most difficult moments."

—Wangari Maathai

"Great things are not done by impulse, but by a series of small things brought together."

—Mary Anne Evans

"The most courageous act is still to think for yourself. Aloud."

—Coco Chanel

"If you wish to heal your sadness or anger, seek to heal the sadness or anger of others. They are looking to you for guidance, help, courage, strength, understanding, and for assurance. Most of all, they are looking to you for love."

—Ana Castillo

Chapter Eight

August:
Sing Your Songs of Strength

"I am not afraid. I was born to do this."

—Joan of Arc

"We don't develop courage by being happy every day. We develop it by surviving difficult times and challenging adversity."

—Barbara De Angelis

"Courage is not the absence of fear. Courage is the recognition that some things are more important than fear—and what's more important to me is faith."

—Irshad Manji

"Stay afraid, but do it anyway. What's important is the action. You don't have to wait to be confident. Just do it, and eventually the confidence will follow."

—Carrie Fisher

"You may not always have a comfortable life, and you will not always be able to solve all of the world's problems at once, but don't ever underestimate the importance you can have, because history has shown us that courage can be contagious and hope can take on a life of its own."

—Michelle Obama

213
Slow to Faith, Quick to Prayer

My coming to faith
did not start with a leap
but rather a series of staggers
from what seemed like one safe
place to another.
Like lily pads, round and green,
these places summoned and then
held me up while I grew.
Each prepared me for the next leaf
on which I would land,
and in this way I moved across
the swamp of doubt and fear.

—Anne Lamott

214
Riding the Karmic Wave

There are the waves
and there is the wind,
seen and unseen forces.
Everyone has these same elements
in their lives, the seen and unseen:
karma and free will.
The question is,
'how are you going to handle what you have?'
You are riding the karmic wave
underneath and the wind can shift.

Everyone must take what they see
and deal with that which is unseen.

—Kuan Yin

215

If You Want to Change Your Life, You Must Learn This

Patience is the key.
Patience.
If you learn nothing else from meditation,
You will learn patience.
Patience is essential
For any profound change.

—Henepola Gunaratana

216

Now Comes the Turning of the Tide

When you get into a tight place
And everything goes against you,
Till it seems as though you could not
Hang on a minute longer,
Never give up then,
For that is just the place and time
That the tide will turn.

—Harriet Beecher Stowe

217

Wisdom and Strength

Dear God,
I have many problems in my life
That I don't know the answer to,
But I trust that you do.
Please guide me in the way
That is best and gives me wisdom and strength.
May your will be done! Amen.

—Katrina Brohn

218

Look to Tomorrow

With the new day comes new strength and new thoughts.

—Eleanor Roosevelt

219

Learning Who You Really Are

You may encounter many defeats,
But you must not be defeated.
In fact, it may be necessary
To encounter the defeats,
So you can know who you are,
What you can rise from,
How you can still come out of it.

—Maya Angelou

220

Make Me Strong in Spirit

Make me strong in spirit
Courageous in action
Gentle of heart
Let me act in wisdom
Conquer my fear and doubt
Discover my own hidden gifts
Meet others with compassion
Be a source of healing energies
And face each day with hope and joy

—Abby Willowroot, silversmith and priestess

221

A Prayer to Our Heavenly Father to Follow St. Joan of Arc's Example

O, mighty Lord, I pray
That You will be my shield,
just as You protected St. Joan of Arc in battle.

—Eighteenth Century Schoolgirl Prayer

222

I Found God in Myself and I Loved Her Fiercely

I was missing something
a laying on of hands
not a man

---

laying on
not my mama/holding me tight/saying
I'm always gonna be her girl
not a laying on of bosom and womb
a laying on of hands
the holiness of myself released
I sat up one nite walking a boarding house
screaming/crying/the ghost of another woman
who was missing what I was missing
I wanted to jump up outta my bones
& be done with myself
leave me alone
& go on in the wind
it was too much
I fell into a numbness
til the only tree I cd see
took me up in her branches
held me in the breeze
made me dawn dew
that chill at daybreak
the sun wrapped me up swinging rose light everywhere
the sky laid over me like a million men
I was cold/I was burning up/a child
& endlessly weaving garments for the moon
with my tears
I found god in myself
& I loved her/I loved her fiercely

—Ntozake Shange

223
You Must Do the Thing You Think You Cannot Do

You gain strength, courage, and confidence
By every experience in which
You really stop to look fear in the face.
You are able to say to yourself,
"I lived through this horror.
I can take the next thing that comes along."

—Eleanor Roosevelt

224
Prayer to Heal the Body

Beloved Lord, Almighty God,
Through the Rays of the Sun,
Through the Waves of the Air,
Through the All Pervading Life in Space;
Purify and Revivify Us
And we pray, heal our bodies, hearts, and souls.
Amen.

—Nayaz, Pir-o-murshid Inayat Khan

225

Love Others as You Would Have Them Love You

You and I are One
All of You and Us are One.
All the Souls are One Soul
All the Lights are One Light.

—Messenger of Unity

226

Giving Thanks for All We Are Given

We return thanks to our mother,
the earth, which sustains us.
We return thanks to the rivers and streams
which supply us with water.
We return thanks to all herbs, which furnish medicines
for the cure of our diseases.
We return thanks to the corn, and to her sisters,
the beans and squashes, which give us life.
We return thanks to the bushes and trees,
which provide us with fruit.
We return thanks to the wind,
which, moving the air, has banished diseases.
We return thanks to the moon and the stars,
which have given us their light when the sun was gone.
We return thanks to our grandfather He-no,
that he has protected his grandchildren from witches and reptiles,
and has given us his rain.
We return thanks to the sun,

that he has looked upon the earth with a beneficent eye.
Lastly, we return thanks to the Great Spirit,
in whom is embodied all goodness,
and who directs all things for the good of his children.

—American Indian, Iroquois

227

Bathed in the Milk and Honey

We bathe your palms
In the showers of wine,
In the crook of the kindling,
In the seven elements,
In the sap of the tree,
In the milk and honey,
We place nine pure, choice gifts
In your clear beloved face:
The gift of form,
The gift of voice,
The gift of fortune,
The gift of goodness,
The gift of eminence,
The gift of charity,
The gift of integrity,
The gift of true nobility,
The gift of apt speech.

—Gaelic Chant

228
Acts of Love

This new Bible shall be written
On the hearts of all mankind,
Not by pen or book,
But by acts of Love.
For to Love as She does
Is to truly know who He is.

—Justina M. Pernetter

229
Know That Better Days Are Ahead

Sometimes our best efforts do not go
amiss; sometimes we do as we meant to.
The sun will sometimes melt a field of sorrow
that seemed hard frozen; may it happen for you.

—Anonymous

230
We Are Here to Love 24/7

Start the Day with Love;
Spend the Day with Love;
Fill the Day with Love;
End the Day with Love;
This is the way to God.

—Bishop Kim Davis

231
Exult in Each Morning

There is joy
in all:
in the hair I brush each morning,
in the Cannon towel, newly washed,
that I rub my body with each morning,
in the chapel of eggs I cook
each morning,
in the outcry from the kettle
that heats my coffee
each morning,
in the spoon and the chair
that cry, "Hello there, Anne,"
each morning,
in the godhead of the table
that I set my silver, plate, cup upon
each morning.
All this is God,
right here in my pea-green house
each morning
and I mean,
though often forget,
to give thanks,
to faint down by the kitchen table
in a prayer of rejoicing
as the holy birds at the kitchen window
peck into their marriage of seeds.
So while I think of it,

let me paint a thank-you on my palm
for this God, this laughter of the morning,
lest it go unspoken.
The joy that isn't shared, I've heard,
dies young.

—Anne Sexton

232
Keep on the Sunny Side of Life

Keep on the sunny side, always on the sunny side,
Keep on the sunny side of life;
It will help us every day, it will brighten all the way,
If we keep on the sunny side of life.
Tho' the storm in its fury break today,
Crushing hopes that we cherished so dear,
Storm and cloud will in time pass away,
The sun again will shine bright and clear.
Keep on the sunny side, always on the sunny side,
Keep on the sunny side of life;
It will help us every day, it will brighten all the way,
If we keep on the sunny side of life.
Let us greet with a song of hope each day,
Tho' the moments be cloudy or fair;
Let us trust in our Savior always,
Who keepeth everyone in His care.
Keep on the sunny side, always on the sunny side,
Keep on the sunny side of life;

It will help us every day, it will brighten all the way,
If we keep on the sunny side of life.

—Ada Blenkhorn, 1899

233

We Are Guarded, Guided, and Protected

The light of God surrounds us;
The love of God enfolds us;
The power of God protects us

—Unity Church Song

234

There Is a Balm in Gilead

There is a balm in Gilead
To make the wounded whole;
There is a balm in Gilead
To heal the sin-sick soul.
Sometimes I feel discouraged,
And think my work's in vain,
But then the Holy Spirit
Revives my soul again.
There is a balm in Gilead
To make the wounded whole;
There is a balm in Gilead
To heal the sin-sick soul.
If you can't preach like Peter,
If you can't pray like Paul,

Just tell the love of Jesus,
And say He died for all.
There is a balm in Gilead
To make the wounded whole;
There is a balm in Gilead
To heal the sin-sick soul.

—African American Spiritual

235
His Love Is Like the Warmth of the Sun

The Lord bless you and keep you;
The Lord make his face shine upon you and be gracious to you;
The Lord turn his face toward you and give you peace.

—Numbers 6:24–26

236
Each Day Is a Gift

Thank you, dear God, for the morning,
Thank you, dear God, for the day.
Thank you, dear God, for everything—
That's all I have to say!

—Sandi Kimmel

237
The Prayer Wheel

If you're hungry, pray. If you're tired,
Pray to Gandhi and Dorothy Day.
Shakespeare. Sappho. Sojourner Truth.
Pray to the angels and the ghost of your grandfather.
And if you are riding on a bicycle
or a skateboard, in a wheelchair, each revolution
of the wheels a prayer that as the earth revolves
we will do less harm, less harm, less harm.

—Ellen Bass

238
Heal the World!

Our children who live on earth,
Holy are each and every one of you.
May good dreams come,
Your way be found,
And heaven and earth rejoice with you.

—Mile High Healers Group, Denver

239
The Lesson in Letting Go

You will find that it is necessary to let things go;
simply for the reason that they are heavy.
So let them go, let go of them.
I tie no weights to my ankles.

—C. JoyBell C.

240
Finding the Treasure Within

Looking behind,
I am filled with gratitude.
Looking forward,
I am filled with vision.
Looking upwards,
I am filled with strength.
Looking within,
I discover peace.

—Native American Proverb

241
Finding Peace in the River of Tears

Blessed be the story-tellers, music-makers, and artists at life,
for they are the true light of the world.
Blessed be the tender-hearted who mourn and grieve

the wars we've fought, the lives we've lost,
may peace ride in on the river of their tears.

—Jan Phillips

242

Be a Blessing to Those on Your Way

May your walking be easy, on dry land or snow.
May the good Lord walk with you, wherever you go.
May your troubles brush off, like a sprinkling of dust,
And may you stand strong, for what is good, what is just.
May your soul be always grateful, may joy fill your heart.
May you reach out to others, with love, from the start.
May friendships bring blessing, for you, every day.
And may you be a blessing to those on your way.

**—Retired Episcopal Priest Rev. Jane R. Dunning, Diocese
of Western Massachusetts; Chaplain, Shelburne Falls
Fire Departments**

243

Lord's Gift of Power Who Fulfils Our Desire

Awake, O powerhouse of faith,
Awake, O woman you are born to take,
that God has bestowed upon,
Everything God has filled in your heart,
The tremendous power to win the hearts,
The amazing shower of love that you inspire,
And the unbelievable art of making everything true,

Unlock the power that God has given you,
Prove your worth, prove your existence,
This one is an opportunity to make it a truth.

—Jaya Khan

244

See the Sacred in Every Sunset

My god is all gods in one.
When I see a beautiful sunset,
I worship the god of Nature;
when I see a hidden action brought to light,
I worship the god of Truth;
when I see a bad man punished
and a good man go free,
I worship the god of Justice;
when I see a penitent forgiven,
I worship the god of Mercy.

—Edna St. Vincent Millay

245

Extraordinary Ordinary

If I could give you information of my life, it would be to show how a
woman of very ordinary ability has been led by God in strange and
unaccustomed paths to do In His service what He has done in her.
And if I could tell you all, you would see how God has done all, and
I nothing.

—Florence Nightingale

Our Experiences Make Us Who We Are

"Now that I knew fear, I also knew it was not permanent. As powerful as it was, its grip on me would loosen. It would pass."

—Louise Erdrich

"I've been absolutely terrified every moment of my life—and I've never let it keep me from doing a single thing I wanted to do."

—Georgia O'Keeffe

"I do believe in the old saying, 'What does not kill you makes you stronger.' Our experiences, good and bad, make us who we are. By overcoming difficulties, we gain strength and maturity."

—Angelina Jolie

"Never bend your head. Always hold it high. Look the world straight in the eye."

—Helen Keller

Chapter Nine

September:
Faith, Hope, and Love

"Not truth, but faith, it is that keeps the world alive."

—Edna St. Vincent Millay

"Blessed is she who believed that the Lord would fulfill His promises to her."

—Luke 1:45

"Hope begins in the dark, the stubborn hope that if you just show up and try to do the right thing, the dawn will come. You wait and watch and work: you don't give up."

—Anne Lamott

"God is within her, she will not fall."

—Psalm 46:5

" 'Twasn't me, 'twas the Lord! I always told Him, 'I trust to you. I don't know where to go or what to do, but I expect You to lead me,' an' He always did."

—Harriet Tubman

246

Novena in Honor of Saint Anne

Glorious Saint Anne, I desire to honor you with a special devotion.
I choose you, after the Blessed Virgin, as my spiritual mother and
protectress. To you I entrust my soul and my body and all my
spiritual and temporal interests, as well as those of my family.

—Catholic Liturgy

247

The Divine Path of Abundance

Continue down the path that makes you feel fulfilled.
Following one's heart,
continuing on one's divine path can bring abundance.

—Kuan Yin

248

Deep Rest

May the gentleness of God's supportive
and sustaining love
gather us in her arms this day/night,
and bless us with sleep that restores both body and soul. Amen.

—Marchiene Vroon Rienstra

249
Bathe in the River of Healing

For those who have no voice,
we ask you to speak.
For those who feel unworthy,
we ask you to pour your love out
in waterfalls of tenderness.
For those who live in pain,
we ask you to bathe them
in the river of your healing.
For those who are lonely, we ask
you to keep them company.
For those who are depressed,
we ask you to shower upon them
the light of hope.

—Maya Angelou

250
Hymn to Time

Time is being
and being time, it is all one thing,
the shining, the seeing,
the dark abounding.

—Ursula K. Le Guin

251
You Can Heal Yourself

You have the power to heal yourself,
and you need to know that.
We think so often that we are helpless
but we're not.
We always have the power of our minds.
Claim and consciously use your power.

—Louise Hay

Prayer Practice: Reading Sacred Texts

Most religions have a holy book or books that one can look to for inspiration or in times of need, but these aren't the only texts that can be sacred! Many people find spiritual meaning in certain novels and poems, and rereading them can bring inspiration and self-discovery. This could also be said of books on theology, collections of sermons, and prayer books. Try reading any of these or even texts that aren't from your own faith to help strengthen and understand your beliefs and yourself!

252

Keep Looking for Those Silver Linings

If you want the rainbow, you have to put up with the rain.

—Dolly Parton

253

Be Calm in Your Heart

Peace.
It does not mean to be in a place
where there is no noise,
trouble, or hard work.
It means to be in the midst
of those things and still be calm in your heart.

—Unknown

254

Boundaries Are Beautiful

Love yourself enough to set boundaries.
Your time and energy are precious.
You get to choose how you use it.
You teach people how to treat you
by deciding what you will and won't accept.

—Anna Taylor

255

Help Those Who Are Troubled and Anxious

Brigid, you were a woman of peace,
You brought harmony where there was conflict.
You brought light to the darkness.
You brought hope to the downcast.
May the mantle of your peace
cover those who are troubled and anxious,
And may peace be firmly rooted in our hearts and in our world.

—St. Brigid Psalm

256

Up-Hill

Does the road wind up-hill all the way?
Yes, to the very end.
Will the day's journey take the whole long day?
From morn to night, my friend.
But is there for the night a resting-place?
A roof for when the slow dark hours begin.
May not the darkness hide it from my face?
You cannot miss that inn.
Shall I meet other wayfarers at night?
Those who have gone before.
Then must I knock, or call when just in sight?
They will not keep you standing at that door.
Shall I find comfort, travel-sore and weak?
Of labour you shall find the sum.

Will there be beds for me and all who seek?
Yea, beds for all who come.

—Christina Rossetti, 1830–1894

257

Those Special Graces

Saint Catherine Labouré, you were the chosen confidant of the
Blessed Virgin Mary. She revealed to you her desire that her
children wear the Miraculous Medal as a mark of their love for
her and in honor of her Immaculate Conception. Intercede for us,
that we may follow our heavenly mother's desires. Ask that we may
receive those special graces which flow from her motherly hands
like rays of light. Amen.

—Prayer to St. Catherine

258

Strength and Shield

The Lord is my strength and my shield;
my heart trusts in him, and he helps me.
My heart leaps for joy,
and with my song I praise him.

—Psalm 28:7

259

The Stillness of the Stars Guard You

May the peace of the tallest mountain
and the peace of the smallest stone
be your peace.
May the stillness of the stars watch over you.
May the everlasting music of the wave lull you to rest.

—Celtic Blessing Prayer

260

Hope and Constancy

Good St. Dymphna, you placed all your hope in Christ's promises,
and sacrificed even your life in that hope. The Lord, God,
rewarded your constancy by making your name known and loved
over many centuries by the thousands whom you have aided in
time of difficulty. Please assist us now in our present necessity and
intercede before God for our intentions. Obtain for us a firm hope
like your own in God's unfailing protection. Amen.

—Good Shepherd Ministry

261

Grateful for My Chance to Grow

Sky above me Earth below me
flying swirling through the all
seeds of love are growing in me
all of nature blooms along

grace and joy I am unfolding
grateful for my chance to grow

—Lizabeth Gottsegen

262

Calm My Fears and Worries

Dear Lord, I am so thankful that I don't have to worry about the
ways of this world. Help me to trust your ways. When I find myself
trying to control things in life, help me to remember your will be done.
When I am self-absorbed with life's many responsibilities and struggle
to find a clear frame of mind, please send your Holy Spirit to calm my
fears and worries. Amen.

—April Richter

263

All Things Great and Small

Lord, grant that I may always allow myself
to be guided by you, always follow your plans,
and perfectly accomplish your holy will.
Grant that in all things, great and small,
today and all the days of my life,
I may do whatever you may require of me.
Help me to respond to the slightest prompting
of your grace so that I may be your trustworthy
instrument, for your honor.

May your will be done in time and eternity,
by me, in me, and through me. Amen.

—Plea by St. Teresa of Avila

264
Your Promises

Lord, thank you for giving us hope
even in our times of suffering.
Help us to praise you in all circumstances,
just as you will for us in Christ Jesus.
Help our praise for you reflect the confidence
we have in your promises.
And may our praise in turn lead others to your grace.
In Jesus' name, Amen.

—Brooke King

265
The Hand of a Friend to Hold When You Need It

May there always be work for your hands to do
May your purse always hold a coin or two
May the sun always shine upon your window pane
May a rainbow be certain to follow each rain
May the hand of a friend always be near to you, and
May God fill your heart with gladness to cheer you.

—Irish Blessing

266

Prayer of a Sixteen-Year-Old Girl

Loving and believing in your goodness
I thank you for the beauty put before me.
Asking for serenity and acceptance
I will have the courage to grow.
Giving to and respecting all others
May the world be closer to peace.

—Maggie Shaw

267

Lay Down Your Burdens

I cast
every burden
on the Christ within
and I go free!

—Florence Scovel Shinn, 1925

268

Sacred Words of the Earth

It is lovely indeed, it is lovely indeed.
I, I am the spirit within the earth…
The feet of the earth are my feet…
The legs of the earth are my legs…
The bodily strength of the earth is my strength…
The thoughts of the earth are my thoughts…

The voice of the earth is my voice...
The feather of the earth is my feather...
All that belongs to the earth belongs to me...
All that surrounds the earth surrounds me...
I, I am the sacred words of the earth...
It is lovely indeed, it is lovely indeed.

—Navajo Chant

269
In the Stillness of the Starry Night

In the joy of your heart,
Your light remains
In the gift of your caring,
Your light remains
Where you reached out to help,
Your light remains
Where you sat in silent peace,
Your light remains
In the place where you worked,
Your light remains
In the stillness of the starry night,
Your light remains
In the light of each day fully embraced,
Your light remains
Like the touch of an Angel,
Your light remains
When you live as a light,

Your heart is joined in the Infinite Light of Love.
And that about you which is eternal…*remains.*

—Reverend Jacquie Riker

270

Believe in the Good, Even in the Hardest Times

I believe in the sun
though it is late in rising.
I believe in love
though it is absent.
I believe in God
though He is silent.

—ruth weiss, Poet and Holocaust Survivor

271

Keep Looking for the Open Doors

When one door of happiness closes,
another opens,
but often we look so long
at the closed door
that we do not see the one
that has been opened for us.

—Helen Keller

272
Quiet Confidence

The Lord's justice will dwell in the desert,
his righteousness live in the fertile field.
The fruit of that righteousness will be peace;
its effect will be quietness and confidence forever.

—Isaiah 32:16–17

273
Goodness Is Everywhere

I had, a few days ago, an insight which consoled me very much.
It was during my thanksgiving, when I make
a few reflections upon the goodness of God, and
how should one not think of this at such a time, of that
infinite goodness, uncreated goodness, the source of all goodness....
I saw written as in letters of gold this word "Goodness"
which I repeated for a long time with indescribable sweetness.
I beheld it, I say, written upon all creatures, animate and inanimate,
rational or not, all bore this name goodness....
I understood then that all these creatures have of goodness and
all the services and assistance that we receive from each of them
is a benefit which we owe to the goodness of God
who has communicated to them something of his infinite goodness
so that we may meet it in everything and everywhere.

—St. Thérèse Couderc, 1865

274
Every Single Day Is a Miracle

Each day is a blessing
of epic proportions.
I give thanks for
what might seem meager comforts:
real cream in my coffee,
a day without a bill in the mail,
the Paso Doble.
Sometimes life is a dance
a woman has to do backwards
pushing against the wind
and obstacles in the way.
Thank You for being the partner
who always leads.

—Ruth Williams

275
A Child's Gratitude

Goodnight God.
I hope you are having
a good time being the world.
I like the world very much.
I'm glad you made the plants
and trees survive with the
rain and summers.
When summer is nearly near
the leaves begin to fall.

I hope you have a good time
being the world.
I like how God feels around
everyone in the world.
God, I am very happy that
I live on you.
Your arms clasp around the world.
I like you and your friends.
Every time I open my eyes
I see the gleaming sun.
I like the animals—the deer,
and us creatures of the world,
the mammals.
I love my dear friends.

—Dee Baxter

276

Pour the Balm of Peace on This World

Dear Creator, You, the borderless
sea of substance, we ask you to give to all the
world that which we need most—Peace.

—Maya Angelou

Experience Is Life's Best Teacher

"Life is the only real counselor; wisdom unfiltered through personal experience does not become a part of the moral tissue."

—Edith Wharton

"These are the soul's changes. I don't believe in aging. I believe in forever altering one's aspect to the sun. Hence my optimism."

—Virginia Woolf

"Greatness is not measured by what a man or woman accomplishes, but by the opposition he or she has overcome to reach his goals."

—Dorothy Height

"Do what you can! If you can't feed one hundred people, then feed just one."

—Mother Teresa (St. Teresa of Calcutta)

Chapter Ten

October:
To Strengthen and to Heal

"Take chances, make mistakes. That's how you grow. Pain nourishes your courage. You have to fail in order to practice being brave."

—Mary Tyler Moore

"I have learned over the years that when one's mind is made up, this diminishes fear; knowing what must be done does away with fear."

—Rosa Parks

"If we greet situations with a positive attitude, we will eventually create positive returns. If we respond with a negative attitude, negative things will eventually come our way."

—Tenzin Palmo

"The sufferer who keeps looking for God has, in the end, privileged knowledge... She passes through a door that only pain will open, and is thus qualified to speak of God in a way that others, whom we generally call more fortunate, cannot speak."

—Ellen F. Davis

277

Stronger Than the Storm Within Me

I will trust in the
darkness and know that my
times, even now, are in Your
hand. Tune my spirit to the
music of heaven, and
somehow, make my
obedience count for You.

—The Prayer of St. Brendan

278

Find Refuge Here

He will cover you with his feathers,
and under his wings you will find refuge;
his faithfulness will be your shield and rampart.
You will not fear the terror of night,
nor the arrow that flies by day,
nor the pestilence that stalks in the darkness,
nor the plague that destroys at midday.

—Psalm 91:1–16

279

Prayer to Become Pregnant

Dear loving heavenly Father,
I am Your child and I long

to have a child of my own in my
arms—a child to love and to cherish
for the rest of my life, just as You have
loved me with Your everlasting love.
Whatever the reason, Lord, that I have not
conceived, I pray, Lord, that You would
give me the strength to get pregnant and
bear a little baby, just as Sarah
in the Old Testament was given the grace to
conceive and bear her son, Isaac…
Thank You, Lord, for hearing
my prayer, and I leave my life in Your
hands; in Jesus' name I pray, Amen.

—Sanctuary of the Sands

280
A Prayer for the Good of All People

Let us pray for all to be happy,
to love one another,
to help each other,
to gain wisdom,
for all to receive god's blessings,
to break free from the illusion
that is distracting us from our true nature.
No one shall go hungry,
no one will suffer,
abundance is with everyone
and all negativity shall be removed!

—Unitarian Universalist Blessing

281
Wish for Women with Breast Cancer

Father, for the strength you have given me, I thank you.
For the health you have blessed me with, I thank you.
For the women who are going through breast cancer and their families
I ask you to strengthen and to heal them as you see fit.
Lord, we know you want us to be in good health and to prosper.
Lord, use us to do the work you have for us to do
For we know time is getting short on this earth.
Lord, be with every woman who is sick
and encourage them as only you can.
I know how faithful you are.
You have shown yourself to be everything
you say you are in your Holy Word.
I praise you, for you made this body
and you can heal this body.
In Jesus' name I pray.
Amen.

—Breast Cancer Clinic of Barboursville

282
Comfort for My Mother

Loving Lord and Father of all comfort,
I come to You in the name of Jesus
to lay my mother at your feet,
knowing that she has been so unwell
for such a long time. I ask, Lord, that
You heal her of whatever it is that is troubling her.

Free her, I pray, from the pain and confusion
she is going through and restore her to full health
and strength, for You are the God Who heals and cares.
Help my dear mother speedily I pray,
and we will give you all the
praise and glory due to Your name. Amen.

—Mission United

283

Shine Your Love Down

All the cattle are resting in the fields,
The trees and the plants are growing,
The birds flutter above the marshes,
Their wings uplifted in adoration,
And all the sheep are dancing,
All winged things are flying,
They live when you have shone on them.

—Ancient Egyptian Ode to the Sun

Prayer Practice: Smoke and Fire

Fire and smoke have been used for ages in many religious and secular rituals around the world and can have different purposes and intentions. Some fire ceremonies have symbolic meanings (lighting an eternal flame, a menorah, or a prayer candle); some are used for blessing or cleansing (Native American smudging and Pagan smoke cleansing); and some are used for sacrifices, offerings, and new beginnings (Hindu Homa, Yajna, and even the burning of pictures of ex-boyfriends like you see on sitcoms). In ancient times, people would also burn food and wine, and the smoke was sent up as an offering to the gods. Like water, fire is an element that has many spiritual connections, so incorporating even something small like burning a candle or incense into your prayer practice can help strengthen your prayer's intention.

284
Hope and Healing for Dear Mother

Dear Lord, my lovely mom has become quite poorly and is now in hospital.

Lord, I pray that You give the doctors and nurses the knowledge, skill, and wisdom to give her the treatment that she needs to restore her to health and strength, and I ask that You graciously minimize any pain that she may have. Lord, I know that our times and our health are in Your hands, but I also know that You are a God Who can do miracles today, and I do ask on behalf of my dear mom that You would raise her up and restore her heath to her, and we will give You all the praise and all the glory. In Jesus' name we pray. Amen.

—Kaiser Hospital Chapel

285
A Prayer for Those Who Are Dealing with Alzheimer's Disease

Dear Lord,
For the many persons who have died
of Alzheimer's Disease, we pray that
they are in the care of your loving arms…
For those who are now victims of Alzheimer's
Disease, we pray for dignity and comfort…
For the Alzheimer's Disease caregivers,
we pray for compassion and patience…
For the Alzheimer's Disease families,
we pray for strength and courage…
For those who seek the cause, cure,
prevention, and treatment of Alzheimer's
Disease, we pray for your wisdom, guidance,
and direction and

For the hope You have given us…
our thanks. Amen.

—Grace Hospice

286
Prayer for a Baby's Chronic Illness

Father, we bow before You in reverence and fear, asking for Your
healing touch on the life of this little child. We are concerned, Lord,
about this chronic illness and pray that in Your grace and mercy this
little baby might be quickly healed and speedily nursed back into full
health and strength. Comfort this little one, and ease the suffering and
discomfort that they are going through; we pray that the distressing
symptoms of this chronic sickness would soon be reduced and that
the baby returns to normal health in every part of their body. Give
the doctors the wisdom to treat this illness correctly and quickly.
Strengthen and help the parents and all who are involved in the
nursing care, and give them all they may need to continue to look
after such a sick child…and I pray that I may be able to lay all of their
worries and concerns down at Your feet—knowing that You are the
God Who cares for little children and You are a God Who heals. May
Your peace that passes understanding guard the hearts of the parents
in the days that lie ahead, and we will give You all the praise and all the
glory, Amen.

—Carmel By the Sea Chapel

287
Only Trust

All shall
be well,
and all shall
be well,
and all manner
of things
shall be well.

—Julian of Norwich, Fourteenth Century

288
Prayer for a Parent Suffering the Darkness of Mental Illness

Dear Lord, my mother is really struggling. Her depression (bipolar disease, anxiety, paranoia) is really causing her such deep darkness. I know you know her from her mother's womb. I know you know the wounds she has suffered and the terrible things which have scarred her. The illness itself has so shaken her and wounded her relationships with so many others. I confess that I have lost my patience and have not been kind to her. It is difficult to remember that she is suffering from a disease. She isn't being difficult on purpose. She pushes me away, and I become defensive, even angry at her. Give me the grace to see her woundedness and to love her with your own compassion. Accompany her, dear Jesus, in her suffering. May she find some relief with the help of the right care. May I be different in loving her with greater tenderness and understanding. May even momentary times of connection be blessings for each of us. Someday, I know we will both free and with you in your embrace. I long for the day when she is her best self, knowing and accepting the fullness of your love.

—Anonymous

289
A Prayer for Anxious Times

Take away from me fear, anxiety and distress. Help me to face and endure my difficulty with faith, courage, and wisdom. Grant that this trial may bring me closer to You, for You are my rock and refuge, my comfort and hope, my delight and joy. I trust in Your love and compassion. Blessed is Your name, Father, Son, and Holy Spirit, now and forever, Amen.

—Orthodox Prayer

290
The Hardest Grief: After the Death of a Child

My life is upside down, loving God. The order of the world is out of place, and I can't do anything to right it again. Oh, Lord, you know the pain in my heart at all times, and you know why: my child has died.

How can it be that my beloved child is gone? The child I cared for with such concern in every illness, the one I held close to my heart and promised to take care of for a lifetime, is not here for me to care for anymore. It hurts deeply that I wasn't able to protect this child I love with my whole being from a death that seems so unfair. Be with me in this kind of deep and transformative pain. I now carry this darkness with me on my back and in my heart, always.

Lord, there is not a single minute of my life when this loss is not etched so keenly into my brain and heart, whether it is in the middle of a busy day or in those choking moments of grief in the solitary dark of night. Let me be grateful for every minute we had together. Let me treasure those memories and find joy in them. Help me to deal with people better. They don't know what to say. They stumble and look away when they see me. They pretend nothing has happened. I know they "don't want to remind me," but they don't understand it is with me always, always. Teach me, Lord. Tell me what you want me to do with this. What am I supposed to learn from this kind of pain? What are you calling me to do? Open my battered heart and lead me to comfort and peace. Only you can give me the peace I need. Let me feel your presence in my life.

—**Anonymous**

291
Courage for Life

God, make me brave for life:
oh, braver than this.
Let me straighten after pain,
as a tree straightens after the rain,
Shining and lovely again.
God, make me brave for life;
much braver than this.
As the blown grass lifts,
let me rise

From sorrow with quiet eyes,
knowing Thy way is wise.
God, make me brave, life brings
such blinding things.
Help me to keep my sight;
help me to see aright
that out of dark comes light.

—Unknown

292
Hearts Open Wide

Quick to judge Tempted by drink so many drugs
A prayer for Spirit's link
Our loving planet provides Everything we need
consumerism has died—it was courting greed
Easy to distrust charmed by things
We'll not turn to dust wearing diamond rings
Hearts open wide to All that prevails
We'll flow with the tide on God's ship of sails
We pray for Wisdom to take care of every blade of grass,
Common or rare for Spirit lasts, spirit lasts
For the alcoholic with the golden heart
We pray for freedom from judgment a fresh start
Due to returned cancer that has interrupted ability
We pray for the dancer and our own humility
For the sacrifice of plants, animals and fish
We welcome nourishment to Gaia's dish

For the kindnesses of strangers in Life's many streets
Love is safety—not a danger to the Universal beat

—Georgia Otterson

293
Wish Prayer

Whatever prayer means to you personally,
It is my prayer that you will find what reflect your cries,
Destroy your obstacles; transform your fires into music,
Lead you in times of strife, compel you to action,
And most of all, give you hope.

—Reverend Maggie Oman Shannon

294
Intercession for Those with Breast Cancer Illness

St. Agatha, woman of valor,
from your own suffering we have
been moved to ask your prayers
for those of us who suffer from breast cancer.
We place theses names before you
and ask you to intercede on their behalf.
From where you stand in the health of life eternal,
all wounds healed and all tears wiped away,
pray for [mention your request] and all of us.
Pray God will give us His holy benediction
of health and healing. And we remember
you were a victim of torture and that you learned

firsthand of human cruelty and inhumanity.
We ask you to pray for our entire world.
Ask God to enlighten us with a "genius for
peace and understanding." Ask Him to send us
His Spirit of Serenity, and ask Him to help us
share that peace with all we meet.
From what you learned from your own path of pain,
ask God to give us the Grace we need to remain
holy in difficulties, not allowing our anger or our
bitterness to overtake us. Pray that we will be
more peaceful and more charitable. And from
your holy place in our mystical body, the Church,
pray that we in our place and time will, together,
create a world of justice and peace. Amen.

—St. Agatha Prayer

295
Prayer for a Sick Newborn Baby

Oh Lord Jesus, my little one is not very well at all, and she is so tiny
and vulnerable, and I don't know what to do to help.
Give me wisdom, I pray, and show me what I ought to do.
Lord Jesus, You are the great doctor of all doctors, and You know
exactly what is wrong with her. Lord, I pray that You would
overshadow my little baby and stretch out Your healing hand and
touch her…and make her better very soon I pray.
Grant me peace in my heart and the wisdom to know what I should
do, and help me not to panic but to trust You in all things. I trust You
Lord, Amen.

—Anonymous

296
Prayer Is a Relationship

Prayer is a relationship; half the job is mine. If I want transformation, but can't even be bothered to articulate what, exactly, I'm aiming for, how will it ever occur? Half the benefit of prayer is in the asking itself, in the offering of a clearly posed and well-considered intention. If you don't have this, all your pleas and desires are boneless, floppy, inert; they swirl at your feet in a cold fog and never lift.

—Elizabeth Gilbert

297
Secret Fastness of the Heart

Blessed is the match consumed in kindling flame.
Blessed is the flame that burns in the secret fastness of the heart.
Blessed is the heart with strength to stop its beating for honor's sake.
Blessed is the match consumed in kindling flame.

—Hannah Szenes (a.k.a. Hannah Senesh), World War II Resistance hero, 1944

298
Sacred Web of Life

Creator of heaven and earth,
You are me,
I am you.

—Navajo Maiden, 1929

299

Aging and Saging

By the passing of time
Surely one is in a state of loss
Except those who have faith
And perform righteous deeds
And those who enjoin upon one another.
Abiding by the truth,
Enjoin upon one another steadfastness.

—Dr. Lila Fahlman

300

Live as Though Heaven Is on Earth

Dance as though no one is watching you,
Love as though you have never been hurt before,
Sing as though no one can hear you,
Live as though heaven is on earth.

—Unknown

301

Be Lifted from Your Sorrows

As you leave this place
may the Living Lord go with you;
May he go behind you, to encourage you,
beside you, to befriend you,
above you, to watch over you,

beneath you, to lift you from your sorrows,
within you, to give you the gifts of faith, hope, and love,
and always before you, to show you the way.

—Blair Monie

302

The Healing of Dharma

Assailed by afflictions, we discover Dharma
And find the way to liberation. Thank you, evil forces!
When sorrows invade the mind, we discover Dharma
And find lasting happiness. Thank you, sorrows!
Through harm caused by spirits, we discover Dharma
And find fearlessness. Thank you, ghosts and demons!
Through people's hate, we discover Dharma
And find benefits and happiness. Thank you, those who hate us!
Through cruel adversity, we discover Dharma
And find the unchanging way. Thank you, adversity!
Through being impelled to by others, we discover Dharma
And find the essential meaning. Thank you, all who drive us on!
We dedicate our merit to you all, to repay your kindness.

—Buddhist Benediction

303

Comfort During Trouble

Let us then approach God's throne of grace with confidence, so that
we may receive mercy and find grace to help us in our time of need.

—Hebrews 4:16

We Learn from Women's Stories

"I attribute my success to this—I never gave or took any excuse."

—Florence Nightingale

"It's a long old road, but I know I'm gonna find the end."

—Bessie Smith

"Self-esteem means knowing you are the dream."

—Oprah Winfrey

"I do not think I ever opened a book in my life which had not something to say upon woman's inconstancy. Songs and proverbs all talk of woman's fickleness. But perhaps you will say, these were all written by men."

—Jane Austen

"You know full well as I do the value of sisters' affections: there is nothing like it in this world."

—Charlotte Brontë

Chapter Eleven

November:
Giving Thanks for Family and the Women in Your Life

" 'Thank you' is the best prayer that anyone could say. I say that one a lot. 'Thank you' expresses extreme gratitude, humility, understanding."

—Alice Walker

"She is energetic and strong, a hard worker."

—Proverbs 31:17

"A sister can be seen as someone who is both ourselves and very much not ourselves—a special kind of double."

—Toni Morrison

"Lord, protect them from spiritual and physical attacks on their faith and their family. 'But the Lord is faithful, and he will strengthen you and protect you from the evil one.' "

—2 Thessalonians 3:3

304

Angels to Protect You on Your Way

May all the blessings of our Lord touch your life today.
May He send His little angels to protect you on your way.
Such a wee little fit, sent from above;
Someone so precious to cherish and love.
May sunshine and moonbeams dance over your head
As you quietly slumber in your bed.
May good luck be with you wherever you go
And your blessings outnumber the shamrocks that grow.

—Irish Song

305

A Blessing for Women

Dear Lord, thank you for the woman reading this prayer right now.
Thank you for her heart. May you bless her right now. Fill her with
your incredible peace. Wrap her in your love. May she feel confident
and worthy. I pray that she would grow closer to you every day. May
she face everything with courage, and may she walk in integrity.
Help her with anything she is struggling with, surround her with
encouragement, and give her your precious wisdom. May she
experience joy today in Jesus' name, Amen!

—Jennifer Smith

306
Still She Rises

You may be pushed down.
You may be kept from rising.
But no one can keep you
from lifting your heart
toward heaven.

—Clarissa Pinkola Estés

307
Every Challenge Is Also a Gift

We are alive in a fearsome time,
and we have been given new things to fear.
We've been delivered huge blows but also
huge opportunities to reinforce or reinvent our will.
The easiest thing is to think of returning the blows.
But there are other things we must think about as well,
other dangers we face.
The changes we dread most may contain our salvation.

—Barbara Kingsolver

308
Peace, Love, and Freedom

Do everything with a mind that lets go.
Do not expect any praise or reward.
If you let go a little, you will have a little peace.

If you let go a lot, you will have a lot of peace.
If you let go completely, you will know complete peace and freedom.
Your struggles with the world
will have come to an end.

—Mechaan Chah

309
Oprah's Favorite Prayer

Open your heart and quietly to yourself say the only prayer that's ever needed: Thank you, thank you, thank you. You're still here. You get another chance this day to do better and be better, another chance to become more of who you were created to be and what you're created to fulfill. Thank you. Amen.

—Oprah Winfrey

310
Stand in Your Power

I stand in my own power now, the questions of permission that I used to choke on for my every meal now dead in a fallen heap, and when they tell me that I will fall, I nod. I will fall, I reply, and my words are a whisper my words are a howl I will fall, I say, and the tumbling will be all my own. The skinned palms and oozing knees are holy wounds, stigmata of my She. I will catch my own spilled blood, and not a drop will be wasted.

—Beth Morey

311
Bearing Witness

God, I offer myself to Thee—
to build with me
and to do with me as Thou wilt.
Relieve me of the bondage of self
that I may better do Thy will.
Take away my difficulties
that victory over them may bear witness
to those I would help of Thy Power,
Thy Love, and Thy Way of life.
May I do Thy will always!

—Alcoholics Anonymous' Big Book, 1939

312
Prayer of Gratitude for Mothers

Dear Lord Jesus, thank You for my Mom and for all the love and patience that she has tirelessly given to me throughout my life. I am so grateful for her, and although I don't often show her how much I love her…I do want to thank You with all my heart for blessing me with my dear mother. Amen.

—Anonymous

313
Bless the Children

God, Our Father, we pray that through Your intercession of St. Nicholas you will protect our children. Keep them safe from harm, and help them grow and become worthy in Your sight. Give them strength to keep their Faith in You and to keep alive their joy in Your creation. Through Jesus Christ Our Lord. Amen.

—Cathedral on the Mount

314
Gratitude for My Sister

Thank You, Lord, for my sister and for the wonderful times that we have shared together—thank You that You placed us together in our family and for the privilege of having a sister like mine. Thank You for all that my sister has taught me and the encouragement she has been to me when I have been in time of hardship and distress. Lord, I pray that You would be very close to her and direct and protect her in all she does. May she excel in the fruit of the Spirit and grow in humility and gentleness; and use her in a mighty way to demonstrate the love and grace of the Lord Jesus in all she says and does, in Jesus' name I pray, Amen.

—Baptist Familia

315

Stay on the Bright Side of Life

Let me encourage you to get up every day
and focus on what you do have in life.
Be thankful for the blessings of the little things
even when you don't get what you expect.

—Victoria Osteen

316

The Cathedral of Home

Dearest Lord,
I sit here quietly in my room,
opening my heart to you.
It is so silent! But if I listen intently,
I become aware of the breathing
of my children in beds down the hall.
They sigh softly or move in their beds quietly,
nestled warmly into their dreams.
These most intimate sounds,
coming from the people I love most in the world,
transform this room. It becomes a place
of honoring you, a cathedral of joy and gratitude
toward you for giving me these children.
May I always treasure these gifts you
have given me. In each moment of loving them,
from kisses to laundry to kitchen, may I be
aware of your presence in my life in this way. Thank you!

—Anonymous Mother

317
Prayer of Thanks for My Grandma

How I thank You, heavenly Father, for my dear, dear grandmother.
She has always been such a special support and encouragement to me,
especially as I was growing up and finding out about life and living…
and Lord, she has given me so much of her gentle wisdom and good
advice…never being judgmental, but always fair and kind. Thank You
for the wonderful example she has been throughout my life of a godly
woman who loves Jesus first and foremost, and for the unique way that
she lovingly gently nudges me to turn to You in all the circumstances
of my life. Thank You for placing her in my life. Thank You that I
have had the opportunity of learning so much from her—for her
knowledge of the Scriptures and her delight to turn to You in prayer,
day by day. Lord, now that she is getting older, I pray that You would
keep Your loving arms around her and protect her from harm. Guard
and guide her—protect her and provide all that she needs and draw
her ever closer to Yourself—in Jesus' name I pray, Amen.

—Pine Hill Nazarene Church Member

318
Appreciation for All Mothers-In-Law

We thank You also for the wider family, and today, Lord, we
particularly want to bring before You the role of mothers-in-law
within the family unit. Give grace and wisdom to all women who have
been called into the important role of mother-in-law. This we ask in
Jesus' name, Amen.

—Anonymous

319
A Mother's Prayer for Her Daughter

Loving Lord and heavenly Father, I thank You with all my heart for
this precious daughter of ours.

May she be surrounded by Your peace and protected by Your strength,
and may she find her hope and joy in You alone. Give her ears that are
responsive to Your voice, eyes that look to Jesus as Her Savior, and a
heart that responds to Your grace so that she learns to abide in You
and rests in Your love.

May the time that we spend together be truly blessed by You. I do
praise You, dear Father, for giving me this precious daughter of mine
for this season of our lives—thank You, Father, in Jesus' name I pray,
Amen.

—Moms Circle of San Diego

320
Recovery

The sky is soft as a grandmother's quilt,
fleecy as sheep—sheep as you imagine them to
be, not as they are. The leaves and grass are soft, too.
They seem to heal you with their green fingers,
their heady perfumes rising. The wind will open
its arms, the field will catch you in its lap,
they will rock you, rock you like a baby
as you dreamed it in your deepest longing,
not as it happens when you wish for it
but as it's told in an old, old story,

a story you were born
knowing and later forgot.

—Marcia Falk

321
A Parent's Gratitude for Children

Lord, omnipotent Father, we give you thanks for having given us children. They are our joy, and we accept with serenity the worries, fears, and labors which bring us pain. Help us to love them sincerely.

Give us the wisdom to guide them, patience to teach them, and vigilance to accustom them to the good through our example. Support our love so that we may receive them back when they have strayed and make them good. Grant that they may always see our home as a haven in their time of need. Teach us and help us, O good Father, through the merits of Jesus, your Son and our Lord. Amen.

—Morning Star Advent Church

322
A Mother's Thankful Heart for Her Baby

Heavenly Father, what joy fills my heart for the precious little baby you have seen fit to bring into our family unit. I lift up my voice of praise to You with a grateful heart for this little life that has been entrusted to me. As this little bundle of joy starts to grow and develop, give me wisdom to teach and train—to correct and to encourage; and may I be both fair and wise and combine a balance between correction and encouragement. Guide our little family unit in the ways of peace

I pray, and thank You, my heavenly Father, for the wonderful blessing
that has come from You, Amen.

—Mountain View Moms

323

A Heart Illuminated

My shortest days end,
My lengthening days begin.
What matters more or less sun in the sky,
When all is sun within?

—Christina G. Rossetti

324

Don't Waste Your Happiness

There is no beauty in sadness. No honor in suffering. No growth in
fear. No relief in hate. It's just a waste of perfectly good happiness.

—Katerina Stoykova Klemer

Prayer Practice: Giving, Offering, and Sharing

From charitable acts to sacred gifts offered to deities, offerings are prominent in many religions and are used as a way to become more in touch with one's spirituality. Traditional spiritual and religious offerings often involve giving something specific to a deity in order to invoke the deity for various purposes. This doesn't just involve Pagan altars and ancient blood sacrifices though—other similar practices involve lighting a candle for a deceased loved one at your place of worship or giving alms, as in the practices of Dāna and Zakat. However, at the core of all of these practices is putting intention into a thought or prayer and taking an action involving a material substance to strengthen it. A more modern implementation of this concept could involve giving to charity, opening your home to someone in need, or releasing negative emotions or energies. These and similar actions are believed to contribute positively to your karma and can help you become more in touch with your spirituality, beliefs, or religion.

325
The Kiss of the Sun

The greatest gift
I ever received
was the kiss of the sun
on the days where
I couldn't remember
how to make my own light.

—Unknown

326
Bless This House

Bless this house, O Lord, we pray.
Make it safe by night and day.
Bless these walls so firm and stout,
Keeping want and trouble out.
Bless the roof and chimney tall,
Let thy peace lie over all.
Bless the doors that they may prove
Ever open to joy and love.
Bless the windows shining bright,
Letting in God's heavenly light.
Bless the hearth a-blazing there,
With smoke ascending like a prayer.
Bless the people here within...
Keep them pure and free from sin.

Bless us all, that one day, we
May be fit, O Lord, to dwell with Thee.

—Helen Mary

327

A Child's Prayer for My Mother

Dear Lord Jesus, I love my mom
and thank You for giving me to her.
Thank You for all she does for me
and the food that she makes.
Thank You for giving me the best mom
in the world. Please bless her every day
and help her in all that she does.
Thank You that You died for me on
the cross to forgive me and rose again
so that we can all be with You in heaven.
Please bless us all in Jesus' name, Amen.

—Unity Prayer Hotline

328

Let Me Be a Living Example of Love

Dear Jesus, I confess to you my failures to love.
I thank and praise you for your work of paying
for all those failures, and loving perfectly in my place.
I trust your promise that the Father will give me anything
I ask in your name. I now pray for greater and greater
Christ-like love in all my relationships. Work in me

to bear more and more fruit, to your glory.
In your saving name, I confidently pray. Amen."

—Mollie Schairer

329
When Nursing or Feeding Your Baby

God, you are like a mother to us all,
nourishing all creatures with food and with blessing.
Strengthen my child with (my milk, this food)
and with the warmth of our nearness.

—Nurses of Faith

330
Give Me Wisdom to Teach My Children Well

Lord, please give me the wisdom to make decisions according to your
will. Send me your vision in this situation—and make it plain that I
will see it. And please show me how to teach my child to make wise
decisions so that he/she may also choose the path that is pleasing
to you.

—Bible Club of Ohio Valley

331
Our Hearts as Full

To our Gods of old, we bless the ground
that you tread in search of our freedom!
We bless your presence in our lives and in our hearts!

Take of this offering to your delight,
and be filled with our prayers of thanksgiving!
May our lives remain as full as our hearts on this day!

—Yoruban African Prayer

332
What Comes After the Sadness

Dear God, After the sadness I didn't think I could ever be the same again. I was right. I now have qualities I never had before. I am more sensitive to the sorrows of others. I am more compassionate to the less fortunate. I appreciate deeply. I love more intensely. Thank You for giving me the wisdom that comes from life experiences. Amen.

—Martha Lynn, Harmony Hollow

333
Always Know That You Are Loved

Don't worry, it's going to be OK.
It's all right, little one, you're safe and loved.
It's OK to cry, it's OK to be afraid, it's OK to be weak,
it's OK to be vulnerable, it's OK to be human.
It's from all these elements that we grow,
and it's from all these elements that I am born out of you.
I Love You.

—Anonymous

334
Free Your Heart

Decay your loneliness by making full use
of my greatest gift to mankind, which is mankind.
Feel my alleged absence as proof
of the paradox that I exist and have always existed.
Let me in by letting me out
Love, fear, and all of the other feelings spared
are what create this reality.
These are the cause and effect of compassion and true forgiveness.
Ask for my help in walking through the anguish of forgiveness.
Do everything in your power to learn to forgive
and love those that hurt you,
Not just for them, but for others as well as yourself.
And never give up the hope that someday your ex-suffering
will be able to help the ones who were sick and hurt you,
as well as those who suffered like you.
Learn all this by practicing to love everyone.
If you can learn to love, forgive,
fully listen, understand, and accept those around you,
you will eventually begin to learn how to love, forgive,
fully listen, understand, and accept yourself.

—Anonymous

335
Enter a Joy That Is Free

Flowers, sesame seed, bowls of fresh water, a tuft of kusha grass,
all this altar paraphernalia is not needed
by someone who takes the teacher's words in
and honestly lives them.
Full of longing in meditation,
one sinks into a joy that is free of any impulse to act
and will never enter a human birth again.

—Lalla, Fourteenth Century Indian Mystic

336
The Lord's Work

God,
I'm willing
to do your work.
Please
show me what it is.

—Tami Simon

337

Seeking Goodness All the Days of My Life

I am a woman of valor,
My arms are new with strength.
My hands will plant vineyards;
With dignity will I tend them,
With laughter and with wisdom
will I make them grow;
And I will seek goodness
all the days of my life.

—Proverbs 31

Women Make the World Better

"I trust myself. I trust my instincts. I know what I'm going to do, what I can do, what I can't do. I've been through a lot, and I could go through more, but I hope I don't have to. But if I did, I'd be able to do it."

—Carrie Fisher

"I'm just a small crack in the wall; the wall of patriarchy; on the wall of the hierarchy; on the wall of injustice. Soon there will be more cracks, and someday the wall will fall."

—Dhammanada Bhikkhuni

"Men cannot fulfill God's good purpose for them without the influence of women."

—1 Corinthians 11:11

"Be careful if you make a woman cry, because God counts her tears; every tear a woman sheds is equivalent to man's sacrifices in life. The woman comes from man's rib, not from his feet to be stepped on, not from his head to be superior, but from his side to be equal, under his arms to be protected, and near his heart to be loved."

—The Talmud

Chapter Twelve

December:
A Woman's Spirit

"A woman in harmony with her spirit is like a river flowing. She goes where she will without pretense and arrives at her destination prepared to be herself, and only herself."

—Maya Angelou

"Women's stories are as powerful, inspiring, and terrifying as the goddess herself. And in fact, these are the stories of the goddess. As women, we know her because we are her. Each woman, no matter how powerless she might feel, is a cell within her vast form, an embodiment of her essence, and each woman's story is a chapter in the biography of the sacred feminine."

—Jalaja Bonheim

" 'Nature is woman's best friend,' she [Yasmina] often said. 'If you're having troubles, you just swim in the water, stretch out in a field, or look up at the stars. That's how a woman cures her fears.' "

—Fatema Mernissi

"For each of us as women, there is a deep place within, where hidden and growing our true spirit rises...Within these deep places, each one holds an incredible reserve of creativity and power, of unexamined and unrecorded emotion and feeling. The woman's place of power within each of us...it is dark, it is ancient, and it is deep."

—Audre Lorde

338
Rise up, O Woman

Rise up, O woman,
Get the sword in your hands,
Dare to make your home in the sand,
Take up the challenge to end,
End the struggle that you had,
Unlock the unfathomable power within,
Show to the world the immeasurable potency,
Leave the rest and create the best,
Because that's where you belong to, O woman.

—Persian Poem

339
Tap into Wonder

Rather than fretting about the past or worrying about the
future, the aim is to experience life as it unfolds moment by
moment. This simple practice is immensely powerful. As we
rush through our lives, mindfulness encourages us to stop
constantly striving for something new or better and to embrace
acceptance and gratitude. This allows us to tap into the joy and
wonder in our lives, and to listen to the wisdom of our hearts.

—Anna Barnes

340
I Stand Before You in Prayer

Like the Radiance of the Moon
My God, Creator of beauty and purity
Molder of body and soul,
I am the woman now standing before You in prayer.
Purify me at brooks of water
Anoint me with myrrh and incense
Renew light within me like the radiance of the moon.
My Lord, My womb which You have given me
Is pure; place a soul in my midst.
Then may my home be whole before You,
And my insides be lined with love.

—Ruth Lazare

341
Still I Rise

You will become a graveyard
of all the women you once were
before you rise one morning
embraced by your own skin.
You will swallow a thousand
different names
before you taste the meaning
held within your own.

—Pavana

342
She Weaves the Web of Life

Who is She?
She is your power,
your Feminine source.
Big Mama. The Goddess.
The Great Mystery.
The web-weaver.
The life force.
The first time,
the twentieth time you
may not recognize her.
Or pretend not to hear.
As she fills your body
with ripples of terror and delight.
But when she calls you will know
you've been called.
Then it is up to you to
decide if you will answer.

—Lucy H. Pearce

343
You Are Brave

I am whole.
I am learning.
I am letting go.
I am free.
I am talented and courageous.

I am protecting my joy.
I am brave.
I am healing.
I am loving myself.
Unapologetically.

—Alex Elle

344

The Universe Has Your Back

The universe will bring people whatever they want…
Let the magic happen. It's always there.
Abundance and love are always there.
Believe in the highest good.
There is a higher essence to everything.
The realm you're in has a heaviness that mutes energy.
You can penetrate through it, no matter how dark and heavy.
Sometimes it has nothing to do with karma.
Just don't forget to keep it open.
Don't get too bogged down…
Prosperity can happen at any time.
I want to give you everything that you need.

—Kuan Yin

345
Enough Is a Gift

Be thankful for what you have; you'll end up
having more. If you concentrate on what you don't
have, you will never, ever have enough.

—Oprah Winfrey

346
Listen to the Voice of Your Heart

Woman! Hear the voice and awake!
Mother, O sister, O wife, O woman,
Relinquish what holds you back,
The onus is on your shoulders
To show the right path to those
who have lost their way,
The onus to take forward
the message of God,
Is on your shoulders;
You are the one who
can make the difference,
If you obey the voice of your heart,
You can conquer the doubts that
put you down. For you will
for sure transform,
As with each passing day
God within you increase!

—Hebrew Chant

Prayer Practice: The Divine Feminine

Often times it seems as if many religions focus on men rather than women, but many Pagan religions are centered around goddess worship or only worship female deities. However, anyone can apply the concepts from these religions to their own spiritual or secular lifestyle. The concept of the divine feminine means different things to many different people, but at its core is a respect and appreciation for the strength and feminine powers of women. Celebration of the divine feminine can help women reflect on their strengths in a world that often puts them down, but does not necessarily have to be the traditional worship of a goddess or patron saint. There are many ways to celebrate the divine feminine, like meditating on your own or other women's power of creation, what they have struggled through, and how far they have come in times of trial and hardship. Traditionally, a celebration of the divine feminine involves a gathering of women who have touched your lives to honor and pray for them, so even a girls' night can be turned into a celebration of the divine power women hold, as can saying a prayer for your female ancestors and loved ones or the women you know who are struggling.

347

A Blessing/Prayer While Putting on the Tefillin for Women

May my strength and the power
of my heart be drawn from
the wellsprings of my
Womanhood,
May the sacred fill the earth
From the image of God within me.

—Ayana Friedman

348

Quietness

Help me to find my happiness
in my acceptance of what is my purpose
in friendly eyes, in work well done,
in quietness born of trust.
And most of all
in the awareness of spirit in my being.

—Hebridean Celtic Blessing

349
Heart Full of Love

God, please put a guard at my mouth,
love in my heart
and calm in my mind.
Amen.

—Julie Lepianka

350
Give Us the Strength to Be Peaceful

Great God, who has told us
"Vengeance is mine,"
save us from ourselves,
save us from the vengeance in our hearts
and the acid in our souls.
Save us from our desire to hurt as we have been hurt,
to punish as we have been punished,
to terrorize as we have been terrorized.
Give us the strength it takes
to listen rather than to judge,
to trust rather than to fear,
to try again and again
to make peace even when peace eludes us.

—Joan Chittister, Benedictine Sisters of Erie

351

May All Women Be Respected by Men

Great Spirit, I am Mother.
I was made by You
so that the image of Your love
Could be brought into existence.
May I always carry with me
The sacredness of this honor.
Creator, I am Daughter.
I am the learner of the Traditions.
May I carry them forward
So that the Elders and Ancestors
Will be remembered for all time.
Maker-of-All-Things, I am Sister.
Through me, may my brothers be shown
The manner in which I am to be respected.
May I join with my sisters in strength
and power as a Healing Shield
So that they will no longer bear
the stain of abuse.
Niskam, I am
Committed Partner: One who shares her spirit,
But is wise to remember never to give it away,
Lest it become lost,
And the two become less than one.
I am Woman. Hear me. Welal'in. Ta'ho!

—Native American Chant

352

Prayer Is Listening

Prayer is not asking.
Prayer is putting oneself in the hands of God,
at his disposition,
and listening to his voice in the depths of our hearts.

—Mother Teresa (St. Teresa of Calcutta)

353

Peace Be on Your House

If there is to be peace in the world,
There must be peace in the nations.
If there is to be peace in the nations,
There must be peace in the cities.
If there is to be peace in the cities,
There must be peace between neighbors.
If there is to be peace between neighbors,
There must be peace in the home.
If there is to be peace in the home,
There must be peace in the heart.

—Chinese Poem, 549 AD

354

Protect All Children of the Earth

Creator, open our hearts
to peace and healing between all people.

Creator, open our hearts
to provide and protect for all children of the earth.
Creator, open our hearts
to respect for the earth and all the gifts of the earth.
Creator, open our hearts
to end exclusion, violence, and fear among all.
Thank-you for the gifts of this day and every day.

—**Alycia Longriver, Micmac Tribe**

355

All You Need to Do Is Be Helpful

I am here only to be truly helpful.
I am here to represent Him Who sent me.
I do not have to worry about what to say or what to do,
because He Who sent me will direct me.
I am content to be wherever He wishes, knowing He goes there
with me.
I will be healed as I let Him teach me to heal.

—**A Course in Miracles**

356

Live Life to the Fullest

As you keep your mind and heart focused in the right direction,
approaching each day with faith and gratitude, I believe you will be
empowered to live life to the fullest and enjoy the abundant life He
has promised you.

—**Victoria Osteen**

357

Evening Prayer

May we cooperate with you for genuine justice
and peace in all that we think and say and do.

—Sacred Heart Catholic Church

358

We Are All Meant to Shine

Our deepest fear is not that we are inadequate.
Our deepest fear is that we are powerful beyond measure.
It is our light, not our darkness that most frightens us.
We ask ourselves,
Who am I to be brilliant,
gorgeous, talented, fabulous?
Actually, who are you not to be?
You are a child of God.
We were born to make manifest the glory of God that is within us.
It is not just in some of us; it is in everyone.
And as we let our own light shine, we unconsciously
give other people permission to do the same.
As we are liberated from our own fear,
our presence automatically liberates others.

—Marianne Williamson

359

Prayer for the Right Path

Doing the right thing is our best gift
That is what brings us bliss and happiness.
Happy and blissful is the person who does what is right,
because it is the right thing to do.

—Ancient Zoroastrian Chant

360

Blessings for the Afflicted

I desire neither earthly kingdom,
nor even freedom from birth and death.
I desire only the deliverance from grief
of all those afflicted by misery.
Oh Lord, lead us from the unreal to the real;
from darkness to light;
from death to immortality.
May there be peace in celestial regions.
May there be peace on earth.
May the waters be appeasing.
May herbs be wholesome and
may trees and plants bring peace to all.
May all beneficent beings bring peace to us.
May thy wisdom spread peace all through the world.
May all things be a source of peace to all and to me.
Om Shanti, Shanti, Shanti.

—Patricia Morrison, Crane Dance Collective, 1956

361
Life Is Short, Make the Most of It

Life is like a blink of an eye,
Death is for eternity.
Therefore, life is really just a dream,
And death is the reality.

—Betty Pritchard

362
Be Not Dismayed

Nada te turbe,
Nada te espante,
Toda se pasa,
Dios no se muda,
La Paciencia
Todo la alcanza;
Quien a Dios tiene
Nada le falta,
Sólo Dios basta.

—

Let nothing disturb thee;
Let nothing dismay thee;
All things pass:
God never changes.
Patience attains
All that it strives for.
He who has God

Lacks for nothing:
God alone suffices.

—St. Teresa of Avila, Sixteenth Century

363

How to Pray According to Jesus

Jesus taught that effective prayer must be:
Unselfish—not alone for oneself.
Believing—according to faith.
Sincere—honest of heart.
Intelligent—according to light.
Trustful—in submission to the Father's all-wise will.

—The Urantia Book—144:3

364

The Irresistible Rhythm of Life

Are you lookin' for me?
are you?
are you lookin' for ME?
well you won't find me
'cause I'll be DANCIN'!
I'll be dancin' with the THUNDER
and the IRRESISTIBLE RHYTHM of LIFE!

—Orunamamu, Storyteller

365
Strength in Trouble

As the rain hides the stars,
as the autumn mist
hides the hills,
as the clouds veil
the blue of the sky, so
the dark happenings of my lot
hide the shining of thy face from me.
Yet, if I may hold thy hand in the darkness,
it is enough, since I know
that though I may stumble in my going,
Thou dost not fall.

—Scottish Song

Looking Forward with Newfound Strength

*"I believe every single woman is a Goddess. We are divine,
miraculous, and glorious. It's who we are down to our core. You may
need to rediscover and reclaim this part of yourself, but it's there
just waiting for you to rock it."*

—Alexandra Jaye Johnson

"Goddesses never die. They slip in and out of the world's cities, in and out of our dreams, century after century, answering to different names, dressed differently, perhaps even disguised, perhaps idle and unemployed, their official altars abandoned, their temples feared or simply forgotten."

—Phyllis Chesler

"You don't make progress by standing on the sidelines whimpering and complaining. You make progress by implementing ideas."

—Congresswoman Shirley Chisholm

"I have become my own version of an optimist. If I can't make it through one door, I'll go through another door—or I'll make a door. Something terrific will come no matter how dark the present."

—Joan Rivers

Conclusion

Prayer Is Essential to Your Life

*"Not all of us can do great things.
But we can do small things with great love."*

—Mother Teresa (St. Teresa of Calcutta)

People hunger for ritual, and prayer is one of our most sacred rituals. As children, we create complex rituals of play and interaction. As adolescents, we engage in awkward social rituals to test and define our identities. As adults, we pass certain milestones such as marriage, first house, and first child, yet these traditional milestones reflect only a small portion of the moments we feel ought to be marked in some fashion. This book is filled with blessings for so many aspects of life.

In the twenty-first century, many people feel spiritually adrift as the world moves ever faster. Important events seem to go by unnoticed and unremarked. You can, however, mark these events with the ritual of prayer. You can celebrate the successes, mourn the losses, and shout out the accomplishments. You can design a prayer ritual for family, a community, or just yourself. By doing this, you are providing a sense of connection and a sense of comfort. It strips away the barriers we raise to shield ourselves in everyday life. You can pray in so many ways, and you should; pray in times of difficulty or loss, pray to express gratitude, send a blessing prayer to people across the world, or, on a very personal level, make a prayer that is just between you and God.

Following is the aforementioned guide to starting your own prayer circle. I can tell you that mine has saved my sanity and gotten me through really hard times and seasons of joy as well. I wish the same for you and yours.

Blessing on your house!
Becca Anderson

Prayer Circles

Let's Be Grateful for Each Other and Be Grateful Together

In closing, we thought we would share with you one last way that you can express all of this newfound gratitude, and that is by opening up. The idea is simple. A blessing circle is a place for sharing stories, photos, videos, and prayers of gratitude with friends and loved ones. The more people you can get to align with you, the sooner you will discover the positive power of prayer and reap the many benefits that come from doing so. Now, we want to spread that gift and help you become cheerleaders for others who have tapped into the power of thankfulness by forming your own Power of Prayer Blessings Circle. We make it easy for you with our tips for starting a circle.

Opening to the Power of Prayer

1. As the organizer of the Circle, consider yourself the host or hostess, almost as if you have invited a group of friends—or people you hope will become friends—to your dinner table. Your role is to help guide conversations and serve up a feast—a feast of interesting stories about gratitude or nuggets of information to share that will keep the conversations meaningful and inspiring, and ultimately bring to life the power of gratitude in all the lives of those gathered in your circle.

2. Create a mission or goals for your circle. What do you want to accomplish? How will you manifest this in your own life and the lives of those in your circle? Will you share prayers, stories, inspiring quotes, guided meditations? Create a plan for guiding your group through the practice of Prayer.

3. Decide whether to meet online or in person. The exciting thing about the internet is that you can create a Circle and community online and connect friends and colleagues from across the country—and around the world. See our Facebook page for inspiration. Or you may want to create an in-person circle with friends in your neighborhood or town. I recommend meeting in person, but also Zoom meetings online are very effective and can still feel private. Try a mix of both!

4. Send out evites and invites and make phone calls to invite members to your Circle. Ask everyone to invite a friend and spread the word about your new group.

5. Select a meeting place. Often guides will invite in-person communities to meet at their home. Or you may opt for a local coffee shop or another comfortable meeting place where you can gather regularly.

6. Create a calendar of meetup dates and distribute it to your group.

7. In this book, we have lots of prayers, inspirational quotes, and passages from the Bible to use as prompts for discussions. Please feel free to tap into these resources.

Circles of Grace

These simple suggestions should help you and your Circle get started. Remember, nothing is cast in stone, and you can feel free to improvise until you find your comfort zone. We guarantee you will come away from these gatherings feeling inspired and challenged and with exciting new ideas to share.

First, begin by welcoming your guests. Go around the circle with each person introducing themselves. For example, "I am Sally Smith and I live in Ohio. I am a writer, literacy volunteer, and mother of two." Next read a passage of poetry, a prayer, or quote.

Now, go clockwise around the circle, and ask each participant why she or he is here and what spiritual sustenance he or she is seeking.

Ask a volunteer to read her favorite prayer or quote.

These group gatherings are wonderful, but personal sharing and goal discussion can be intimidating at first, so be mindful of your group, and you'll sense when you will need to wrap things up. Always end on a high note by asking each person to share a prayer story and a blessing to be grateful for. May your transformation be your inspiration!

About the Author

Becca Anderson comes from a long line of teachers and preachers from Ohio and Kentucky. The teacher side of her family led her to become a woman's studies scholar and the author of the bestselling *The Book of Awesome Women*. An avid collector of affirmations, meditations, prayers, and blessings, she helps run a "Gratitude and Grace Circle" that meets monthly at homes, churches, and bookstores in the San Francisco Bay area, where she currently resides. Becca Anderson credits her spiritual practice and daily prayer with helping her recover from cancer and wants to share this encouragement with anyone who is facing difficulty in life with her books *Prayers for Hard Times* and her latest, *Woman's Book of Prayer*.

The author of *Think Happy to Stay Happy* and *Every Day Thankful*, Becca Anderson shares prayers and affirmations, inspirational writings, and suggested acts of kindness at https://thedailyinspoblog. wordpress.com

She blogs about awesome women at:
https://theblogofawesomewomen.wordpress.com/
@AndersonBecca_ on Twitter
@BeccaAndersonWriter on Facebook
@BeccaAndersonWriter on Instagram

Index by Category

CHILDREN

COURAGE

DAUGHTERS

FAITH

GOODNESS

GOD'S LOVE

GRIEF

GROWTH/MOVING FORWARD

HAPPINESS

HOPE

JUSTICE

KINDNESS/COMPASSION

PERSEVERANCE

POTENTIAL

PRAYER

PROTECTION

RELATIONSHIPS

REST

Mango Publishing, established in 2014, publishes an eclectic list of books by diverse authors—both new and established voices—on topics ranging from business, personal growth, women's empowerment, LGBTQ studies, health, and spirituality to history, popular culture, time management, decluttering, lifestyle, mental wellness, aging, and sustainable living. We were recently named 2019 *and* 2020's #1 fastest-growing independent publisher by *Publishers Weekly*. Our success is driven by our main goal, which is to publish high-quality books that will entertain readers as well as make a positive difference in their lives.

Our readers are our most important resource; we value your input, suggestions, and ideas. We'd love to hear from you—after all, we are publishing books for you!

Please stay in touch with us and follow us at:

Facebook: Mango Publishing
Twitter: @MangoPublishing
Instagram: @MangoPublishing
LinkedIn: Mango Publishing
Pinterest: Mango Publishing
Newsletter: mangopublishinggroup.com/newsletter

Join us on Mango's journey to reinvent publishing, one book at a time.